Historical Record Of The Ninety-second Regiment, Originally Termed "the Gordon Highlanders," And Numbered The Hundredth Regiment: Containing An Account Of The Formation Of The Regiment In 1794, And Of Its Subsequent Services To 1850...

Richard Cannon

Nabu Public Domain Reprints:

You are holding a reproduction of an original work published before 1923 that is in the public domain in the United States of America, and possibly other countries. You may freely copy and distribute this work as no entity (individual or corporate) has a copyright on the body of the work. This book may contain prior copyright references, and library stamps (as most of these works were scanned from library copies). These have been scanned and retained as part of the historical artifact.

This book may have occasional imperfections such as missing or blurred pages, poor pictures, errant marks, etc. that were either part of the original artifact, or were introduced by the scanning process. We believe this work is culturally important, and despite the imperfections, have elected to bring it back into print as part of our continuing commitment to the preservation of printed works worldwide. We appreciate your understanding of the imperfections in the preservation process, and hope you enjoy this valuable book.

GENERAL ORDERS.

HORSE-GUARDS,
1st January, 1836.

HIS MAJESTY has been pleased to command that, with the view of doing the fullest justice to Regiments, as well as to Individuals who have distinguished themselves by their Bravery in Action with the Enemy, an Account of the Services of every Regiment in the British Army shall be published under the superintendence and direction of the Adjutant-General; and that this Account shall contain the following particulars, viz.:—

—— The Period and Circumstances of the Original Formation of the Regiment; The Stations at which it has been from time to time employed; The Battles, Sieges, and other Military Operations in which it has been engaged, particularly specifying any Achievement it may have performed, and the Colours, Trophies, &c., it may have captured from the Enemy.

—— The Names of the Officers, and the number of Non-Commissioned Officers and Privates Killed or Wounded by the Enemy, specifying the place and Date of the Action.

a

—— The Names of those Officers who, in consideration of their Gallant Services and Meritorious Conduct in Engagements with the Enemy, have been distinguished with Titles, Medals, or other Marks of His Majesty's gracious favour.

—— The Names of all such Officers, Non-Commissioned Officers, and Privates, as may have specially signalized themselves in Action.

And,

—— The Badges and Devices which the Regiment may have been permitted to bear, and the Causes on account of which such Badges or Devices, or any other Marks of Distinction, have been granted.

By Command of the Right Honorable

GENERAL LORD HILL,
Commanding-in-Chief.

JOHN MACDONALD,
Adjutant-General.

PREFACE.

The character and credit of the British Army must chiefly depend upon the zeal and ardour by which all who enter into its service are animated, and consequently it is of the highest importance that any measure calculated to excite the spirit of emulation, by which alone great and gallant actions are achieved, should be adopted.

Nothing can more fully tend to the accomplishment of this desirable object than a full display of the noble deeds with which the Military History of our country abounds. To hold forth these bright examples to the imitation of the youthful soldier, and thus to incite him to emulate the meritorious conduct of those who have preceded him in their honorable career, are among the motives that have given rise to the present publication.

The operations of the British Troops are, indeed, announced in the "London Gazette," from whence they are transferred into the public prints: the achievements of our armies are thus made known at the time of their occurrence, and receive the tribute of praise and admiration to which they are entitled. On extraordinary occasions, the Houses of Parliament have been in the habit of conferring on the Commanders, and the Officers and Troops acting under their orders, expressions of approbation and of thanks for their skill and bravery; and these testimonials, confirmed by the high honour of their Sovereign's approbation, constitute the reward which the soldier most highly prizes.

It has not, however, until late years, been the practice (which appears to have long prevailed in some of the Continental armies) for British Regiments to keep regular records of their services and achievements. Hence some difficulty has been experienced in obtaining, particularly from the old Regiments, an authentic account of their origin and subsequent services.

This defect will now be remedied, in consequence of His Majesty having been pleased to command that every Regiment shall, in future, keep a full and ample record of its services at home and abroad.

From the materials thus collected, the country will henceforth derive information as to the difficulties and privations which chequer the career of those who embrace the military profession. In Great Britain, where so large a number of persons are devoted to the active concerns of agriculture, manufactures, and commerce, and where these pursuits have, for so long a period, been undisturbed by the *presence of war*, which few other countries have escaped, comparatively little is known of the vicissitudes of active service and of the casualties of climate, to which, even during peace, the British Troops are exposed in every part of the globe, with little or no interval of repose.

In their tranquil enjoyment of the blessings which the country derives from the industry and the enterprise of the agriculturist and the trader, its happy inhabitants may be supposed not often to reflect on the perilous duties of the soldier and the sailor,—on their sufferings,—and on the sacrifice of valuable life, by which so many national benefits are obtained and preserved.

The conduct of the British Troops, their valour, and endurance, have shone conspicuously under great and trying difficulties; and their character has been established in Continental warfare by the irresistible spirit with which they have effected debarkations in spite of the most formidable opposition, and by the gallantry and steadiness with which they have maintained their advantages against superior numbers.

In the official Reports made by the respective Commanders, ample justice has generally been done to the gallant exertions of the Corps employed; but the details of their services and of acts of individual bravery can only be fully given in the Annals of the various Regiments.

These Records are now preparing for publication, under His Majesty's special authority, by Mr. RICHARD CANNON, Principal Clerk of the Adjutant General's Office; and while the perusal of them cannot fail to be useful and interesting to military men of every rank, it is considered that they will also afford entertainment and information to the general reader, particularly to those who may have served in the Army, or who have relatives in the Service.

There exists in the breasts of most of those who have served, or are serving, in the Army, an *Esprit de Corps*—an attachment to everything belonging to their Regiment; to such persons a narrative of the services of their own Corps cannot fail to prove interesting. Authentic accounts of the actions of the great, the valiant, the loyal, have always been of paramount interest with a brave and civilized people. Great Britain has produced a race of heroes who, in moments of danger and terror, have stood "firm as the rocks of their native shore:" and when half the world has been arrayed against them, they have fought the battles of their Country with unshaken fortitude. It is presumed that a record of achievements in war,—victories so complete and surprising, gained by our countrymen, our brothers, our fellow-citizens in arms,—a record which revives the memory of the brave, and brings their gallant deeds before us,—will certainly prove acceptable to the public.

Biographical Memoirs of the Colonels and other distinguished Officers will be introduced in the Records of their respective Regiments, and the Honorary Distinctions which have, from time to time, been conferred upon each Regiment, as testifying the value and importance of its services, will be faithfully set forth.

As a convenient mode of Publication, the Record of each Regiment will be printed in a distinct number, so that when the whole shall be completed, the Parts may be bound up in numerical succession.

INTRODUCTION
TO
THE INFANTRY.

THE natives of Britain have, at all periods, been celebrated for innate courage and unshaken firmness, and the national superiority of the British troops over those of other countries has been evinced in the midst of the most imminent perils. History contains so many proofs of extraordinary acts of bravery, that no doubts can be raised upon the facts which are recorded. It must therefore be admitted, that the distinguishing feature of the British soldier is INTREPIDITY. This quality was evinced by the inhabitants of England when their country was invaded by Julius Cæsar with a Roman army, on which occasion the undaunted Britons rushed into the sea to attack the Roman soldiers as they descended from their ships; and, although their discipline and arms were inferior to those of their adversaries, yet their fierce and dauntless bearing intimidated the flower of the Roman troops, including Cæsar's favourite tenth legion. Their arms consisted of spears, short swords, and other weapons of rude construction. They had chariots, to the axles of which were fastened sharp pieces of iron resembling scythe-blades, and infantry in long chariots resembling waggons, who alighted and fought on foot, and for change of ground, pursuit or retreat, sprang into the chariot and drove off with the speed of cavalry. These inventions were, however, unavailing against Cæsar's legions: in the course of time a military system, with discipline and subordination, was introduced, and British courage, being thus regulated, was exerted to the greatest advantage; a full development of the national character followed, and it shone forth in all its native brilliancy.

The military force of the Anglo-Saxons consisted principally of infantry: Thanes, and other men of property, however, fought on horseback. The infantry were of two classes, heavy and light. The former carried large shields armed with spikes, long broad swords and spears; and the latter were armed with swords or spears only. They had also men armed with clubs, others with battle-axes and javelins.

The feudal troops established by William the Conqueror consisted (as already stated in the Introduction to the Cavalry) almost entirely of horse; but when the warlike barons and knights, with their trains of tenants and vassals, took the field, a proportion of men appeared on foot, and, although these were of inferior degree, they proved stout-hearted Britons of stanch fidelity. When stipendiary troops were employed, infantry always constituted a considerable portion of the military force;

and this *arme* has since acquired, in every quarter of the globe, a celebrity never exceeded by the armies of any nation at any period.

The weapons carried by the infantry, during the several reigns succeeding the Conquest, were bows and arrows, half-pikes, lances, halberds, various kinds of battle-axes, swords, and daggers. Armour was worn on the head and body, and in course of time the practice became general for military men to be so completely cased in steel, that it was almost impossible to slay them.

The introduction of the use of gunpowder in the destructive purposes of war, in the early part of the fourteenth century, produced a change in the arms and equipment of the infantry-soldier. Bows and arrows gave place to various kinds of fire-arms, but British archers continued formidable adversaries; and, owing to the inconvenient construction and imperfect bore of the fire-arms when first introduced, a body of men, well trained in the use of the bow from their youth, was considered a valuable acquisition to every army, even as late as the sixteenth century.

During a great part of the reign of Queen Elizabeth each company of infantry usually consisted of men armed five different ways; in every hundred men forty were "*men-at-arms*," and sixty "*shot;*" the "men-at-arms" were ten halberdiers, or battle-axe men, and thirty pikemen; and the "shot" were twenty archers, twenty musketeers, and twenty harquebusiers, and each man carried, besides his principal weapon, a sword and dagger.

Companies of infantry varied at this period in numbers from 150 to 300 men; each company had a colour or ensign, and the mode of formation recommended by an English military writer (Sir John Smithe) in 1590 was:—the colour in the centre of the company guarded by the halberdiers; the pikemen in equal proportions, on each flank of the halberdiers: half the musketeers on each flank of the pikes; half the archers on each flank of the musketeers, and the harquebusiers (whose arms were much lighter than the muskets then in use) in equal proportions on each flank of the company for skirmishing.* It was customary to unite a number of companies into one body, called a REGIMENT, which frequently amounted to three thousand men: but each company continued to carry a colour. Numerous improvements were eventually introduced in the construction of fire-arms, and, it having been found impossible to make armour proof against the muskets then in use (which carried a very heavy ball) without its being too weighty for the soldier, armour was gradually laid aside by the infantry in the seventeenth century: bows and arrows also fell into disuse, and the infantry were reduced to two classes, viz.: *musketeers*, armed with matchlock muskets,

---

* A company of 200 men would appear thus:—

20 20 20 30 20 30 20 20 20
Harquebuses. Archers. Muskets. Pikes. Halberds. Pikes. Muskets. Archers. Harquebuses.

The musket carried a ball which weighed $\frac{1}{10}$th of a pound; and the harquebus a ball which weighed $\frac{1}{13}$th of a pound.

swords, and daggers; and *pikemen*, armed with pikes from fourteen to eighteen feet long, and swords.

In the early part of the seventeenth century Gustavus Adolphus, King of Sweden, reduced the strength of regiments to 1000 men. He caused the gunpowder, which had heretofore been carried in flasks, or in small wooden bandoliers, each containing a charge, to be made up into cartridges, and carried in pouches; and he formed each regiment into two wings of musketeers, and a centre division of pikemen. He also adopted the practice of forming four regiments into a brigade; and the number of colours was afterwards reduced to three in each regiment. He formed his columns so compactly that his infantry could resist the charge of the celebrated Polish horsemen and Austrian cuirassiers; and his armies became the admiration of other nations. His mode of formation was copied by the English, French, and other European states; but so great was the prejudice in favour of ancient customs, that all his improvements were not adopted until near a century afterwards.

In 1664 King Charles II. raised a corps for sea-service, styled the Admiral's regiment. In 1678 each company of 100 men usually consisted of 30 pikemen, 60 musketeers, and 10 men armed with light firelocks. In this year the King added a company of men armed with hand grenades to each of the old British regiments, which was designated the "grenadier company." Daggers were so contrived as to fit in the muzzles of the muskets, and bayonets, similar to those at present in use, were adopted about twenty years afterwards.

An Ordnance regiment was raised in 1685, by order of King James II., to guard the artillery, and was designated the Royal Fusiliers (now 7th Foot). This corps, and the companies of grenadiers, did not carry pikes.

King William III. incorporated the Admiral's regiment in the second Foot Guards, and raised two Marine regiments for sea-service. During the war in this reign, each company of infantry (excepting the fusiliers and grenadiers) consisted of 14 pikemen and 46 musketeers; the captains carried pikes; lieutenants, partisans; ensigns, half-pikes; and serjeants, halberds. After the peace in 1697 the Marine regiments were disbanded, but were again formed on the breaking out of the war in 1702.*

During the reign of Queen Anne the pikes were laid aside, and every infantry soldier was armed with a musket, bayonet, and sword; the grenadiers ceased, about the same period, to carry hand grenades; and the regiments were directed to lay aside their third colour: the corps of Royal Artillery was first added to the Army in this reign.

About the year 1745, the men of the battalion companies of infantry ceased to carry swords; during

---

* The 30th, 31st, and 32nd Regiments were formed as Marine corps in 1702, and were employed as such during the wars in the reign of Queen Anne. The Marine corps were embarked in the Fleet under Admiral Sir George Rooke, and were at the taking of Gibraltar, and in its subsequent defence in 1704; they were afterwards employed at the siege of Barcelona in 1705.

the reign of George II. light companies were added to infantry regiments; and in 1764 a Board of General Officers recommended that the grenadiers should lay aside their swords, as that weapon had never been used during the Seven Years' War. Since that period the arms of the infantry soldier have been limited to the musket and bayonet.

The arms and equipment of the British Troops have seldom differed materially, since the Conquest, from those of other European states; and in some respects the arming has, at certain periods, been allowed to be inferior to that of the nations with whom they have had to contend; yet, under this disadvantage, the bravery and superiority of the British infantry have been evinced on very many and most trying occasions, and splendid victories have been gained over very superior numbers.

Great Britain has produced a race of lion-like champions who have dared to confront a host of foes, and have proved themselves valiant with any arms. At *Crecy*, King Edward III., at the head of about 30,000 men, defeated, on the 26th of August, 1346, Philip King of France, whose army is said to have amounted to 100,000 men; here British valour encountered veterans of renown:—the King of Bohemia, the King of Majorca, and many princes and nobles were slain, and the French army was routed and cut to pieces. Ten years afterwards, Edward Prince of Wales, who was designated the Black Prince, defeated, at *Poictiers*, with 14,000 men, a French army of 60,000 horse, besides infantry, and took John I., King of France, and his son

Philip, prisoners. On the 25th of October, 1415, King Henry V., with an army of about 13,000 men, although greatly exhausted by marches, privations, and sickness, defeated, at *Agincourt*, the Constable of France, at the head of the flower of the French nobility and an army said to amount to 60,000 men, and gained a complete victory.

During the seventy years' war between the United Provinces of the Netherlands and the Spanish monarchy, which commenced in 1578 and terminated in 1648, the British infantry in the service of the States-General were celebrated for their unconquerable spirit and firmness;* and in the thirty years' war between the Protestant Princes and the Emperor of Germany, the British Troops in the service of Sweden and other states were celebrated for deeds of heroism.† In the wars of Queen Anne, the fame of the British army under the great MARLBOROUGH was spread throughout the world; and if we glance at the achievements performed within the memory of persons now living, there is abundant proof that the Britons of the present age are not inferior to their ancestors in the qualities

---

* The brave Sir Roger Williams, in his Discourse on War, printed in 1590, observes:—" I persuade myself ten thousand of our nation would beat thirty thousand of theirs (the Spaniards) out of the field, let them be chosen where they list." Yet at this time the Spanish infantry was allowed to be the best disciplined in Europe. For instances of valour displayed by the British Infantry during the Seventy Years' War, see the Historical Record of the Third Foot, or Buffs.

† *Vide* the Historical Record of the First, or Royal Regiment of Foot.

which constitute good soldiers. Witness the deeds of the brave men, of whom there are many now surviving, who fought in Egypt in 1801, under the brave Abercromby, and compelled the French army, which had been vainly styled *Invincible*, to evacuate that country; also the services of the gallant Troops during the arduous campaigns in the Peninsula, under the immortal WELLINGTON; and the determined stand made by the British Army at Waterloo, where Napoleon Bonaparte, who had long been the inveterate enemy of Great Britain, and had sought and planned her destruction by every means he could devise, was compelled to leave his vanquished legions to their fate, and to place himself at the disposal of the British Government. These achievements, with others of recent dates, in the distant climes of India, prove that the same valour and constancy which glowed in the breasts of the heroes of Crecy, Poictiers, Agincourt, Blenheim, and Ramilies, continue to animate the Britons of the nineteenth century.

The British Soldier is distinguished for a robust and muscular frame,—intrepidity which no danger can appal,—unconquerable spirit and resolution,—patience in fatigue and privation, and cheerful obedience to his superiors. These qualities, united with an excellent system of order and discipline to regulate and give a skilful direction to the energies and adventurous spirit of the hero, and a wise selection of officers of superior talent to command, whose presence inspires confidence,—have been the leading causes of the splendid victories gained by the British arms.* The fame of the deeds of the past and present generations in the various battle-fields where the robust sons of Albion have fought and conquered, surrounds the British arms with a halo of glory; these achievements will live in the page of history to the end of time.

The records of the several regiments will be found to contain a detail of facts of an interesting character, connected with the hardships, sufferings, and gallant exploits of British soldiers in the various parts of the world where the calls of their Country and the commands of their Sovereign have required them to proceed in the execution of their duty, whether in

---

* " Under the blessing of Divine Providence, His Majesty ascribes the successes which have attended the exertions of his troops in Egypt to that determined bravery which is inherent in Britons; but His Majesty desires it may be most solemnly and forcibly impressed on the consideration of every part of the army, that it has been a strict observance of order, discipline, and military system, which has given the full energy to the native valour of the troops, and has enabled them proudly to assert the superiority of the national military character, in situations uncommonly arduous, and under circumstances of peculiar difficulty."—*General Orders in* 1801.

In the General Orders issued by Lieut.-General Sir John Hope (afterwards Lord Hopetoun), congratulating the army upon the successful result of the Battle of Corunna, on the 16th of January, 1809, it is stated :—" On no occasion has the undaunted valour of British troops ever been more manifest. At the termination of a severe and harassing march, rendered necessary by the superiority which the enemy had acquired, and which had materially impaired the efficiency of the troops, many disadvantages were to be encountered. These have all been surmounted by the conduct of the troops themselves: and the enemy has been taught, that whatever advantages of position or of numbers he may possess, there is inherent in the British officers and soldiers a bravery that knows not how to yield,—that no circumstances can appal,—and that will ensure victory, when it is to be obtained by the exertion of any human means.

active continental operations, or in maintaining colonial territories in distant and unfavourable climes.

The superiority of the British infantry has been pre-eminently set forth in the wars of six centuries, and admitted by the greatest commanders which Europe has produced. The formations and movements of this *arme*, as at present practised, while they are adapted to every species of warfare, and to all probable situations and circumstances of service, are calculated to show forth the brilliancy of military tactics calculated upon mathematical and scientific principles. Although the movements and evolutions have been copied from the continental armies, yet various improvements have from time to time been introduced, to insure that simplicity and celerity by which the superiority of the national military character is maintained. The rank and influence which Great Britain has attained among the nations of the world, have in a great measure been purchased by the valour of the Army, and to persons who have the welfare of their country at heart, the records of the several regiments cannot fail to prove interesting.

THE NINETY-SECOND REGIMENT
(HIGHLANDERS),

BEARS ON THE REGIMENTAL COLOUR AND APPOINTMENTS
THE WORD "EGMONT-OP-ZEE,"
IN COMMEMORATION OF ITS GALLANT CONDUCT IN ACTION ON THE
2ND OCTOBER, 1799;

THE WORD "MANDORA,"
IN CONSIDERATION OF ITS GALLANTRY AND GOOD CONDUCT
ON THE HEIGHTS OF MANDORA, NEAR ALEXANDRIA
ON THE 13TH OF MARCH, 1801;

AND THE SPHINX, WITH THE WORD "EGYPT,"
IN COMMEMORATION OF ITS SERVICES DURING THE CAMPAIGN IN EGYPT
IN THE YEAR 1801;

ALSO THE WORDS,
"CORUNNA,"—"FUENTES D'ONOR,"—"ALMARAZ,"—
"VITTORIA,"—"PYRENEES,"—"NIVE,"—
"ORTHES,"—AND "PENINSULA,"—
IN TESTIMONY OF ITS SERVICES IN SPAIN AND SOUTH OF FRANCE,
FROM 1808 TO 1814;

AND THE WORD "WATERLOO,"
IN HONOR OF ITS DISTINGUISHED CONDUCT
ON THE 18TH OF JUNE 1815.

THE NINETY-SECOND REGIMENT

(HIGHLANDERS).

CONTENTS

OF THE

HISTORICAL RECORD.

Year		Page
1793	INTRODUCTION	1
1794	Letter of Service to the Duke of Gordon, authorizing His Grace to raise a regiment in Scotland	—
——	Appointment of the Marquis of Huntly to be lieut.-colonel commandant . . .	—
——	Establishment of the regiment . . .	2
——	Embodied at Aberdeen, and called *The Gordon Highlanders*	—
——	Embarked from Scotland for Southampton .	—
——	Uniform of the regiment	3
——	Embarked for Gibraltar	—
——	Received its colours at Gibraltar . .	4
1795	Embarked for Corsica	—
——	Inspected by Lieut.-General Thomas Trigge .	—
1796	Reviewed by Lieut.-General Sir Gilbert Eliott .	5
——	Proceeded to Corte to suppress a rebellion .	—
——	Received the thanks of Lieut.-General the Honorable J. T. De Burgh, commanding in Corsica	—

Year		Page
1796	Lieut.-Colonel Commandant the Marquis of Huntly promoted to the colonelcy of the regiment; Major Charles Erskine to be lieut.-colonel; and Captain Alexander Napier to be major	5
——	Expedition against *Porto Ferrajo* in the Isle of Elba	6
——	The British troops withdrawn from Corsica, and returned to Gibraltar	—
——	Received the thanks of the Lieut.-General commanding, on leaving Corsica . . .	7
——	Landed at Gibraltar, and inspected by the Lieut.-Governor	—
——	Holland having leagued with France, declared war against Great Britain. . . .	—
——	Spain also joined France, and declared war .	—
1797	Attempts were made to negociate a peace with France, but did not succeed . . .	8
1798	Regiment embarked for England, and arrived at Portsmouth	—
——	Embarked for Ireland, and arrived at Dublin .	—
——	Serious disturbances took place in Ireland .	9
——	Regiment conveyed in carriages to certain disturbed places	—
——	Encamped in the vicinity of Gorey . .	—
——	Received the thanks of the inhabitants, through the Dean of Ferns, for its conduct .	10
——	Landing of a detachment of French under Gen. Humbert at Bantry Bay	11
——	Surrender of the French and rebel forces to Lieut.-General Lake	—
——	Thanks of Parliament communicated to the troops employed	—
——	The numerical title changed from 100th, to NINETY-SECOND regiment	12

Year		Page
1798	Proceeded into quarters at Athlone	12
——	Bonaparte's invasion of Egypt	—
——	Admiral Nelson's victory over the French fleet in Aboukir Bay	—
——	War declared by the Sublime Porte against France in consequence of the invasion of Egypt	—
——	Co-operation of Russia against France	—
1799	Conjoined expedition of British and Russian forces against the French in Holland	13
——	Regiment marched to Cork for embarkation	—
——	Expression of thanks, and complimentary address from the inhabitants of Athlone on the regiment quitting that garrison	—
——	Embarked at Ramsgate for Holland	14
——	Arrived on the Dutch coast, and advanced to Oude-Sluys	15
——	Engaged the French and Dutch forces under General Brune on the 10th September	—
——	H. R. H. the Duke of York joined and assumed the command of the British and Russian forces on the 14th of September	16
——	Attacked the French at *Alkmaar*	—
——	Retired to former position on the Zuype	—
——	Again engaged the French at *Egmont-op-Zee* on the 2nd of October	—
——	Convention concluded for withdrawing the British and Russian troops from Holland	19
——	Received the Royal authority to bear the word "*Egmont-op-Zee*," on the regimental colour and appointments	—
——	Regiment returned to England	20
——	Proceeded to Chelmsford, and formed in brigade under Major-General Moore	—

Year		Page
1800	Marched to the Isle of Wight, and embarked for the *Isle of Houat* on the coast of France	2
——	Proceeded against *Belle-Isle*	—
——	Returned to the Isle of Houat	—
——	Embarked for Minorca	—
——	Assembled with other corps under the command of General Sir Ralph Abercromby	—
——	Embarked and proceeded to *Cadiz*, but abandoned the enterprise on account of a disease prevailing in that city	—
——	Proceeded to Gibraltar and Minorca, and thence to *Malta*, which had surrendered to Great Britain	22
——	Sailed from Malta to *Egypt* with the expedition under General Sir Ralph Abercromby	—
——	Arrived in Marmorice Bay	—
1801	Proceeded to the Bay of Aboukir	—
——	Landing of the British troops on the 8th of March	—
——	Engagement with the French troops on the heights of *Mandora*, near Alexandria, on the 13th of March	23
——	Lieut.-Colonel Erskine was killed; two captains, six lieutenants (three of them mortally), and two ensigns were wounded; 22 rank and file were killed, and 77 were wounded	24
——	Received the Royal permission to bear the word "*Mandora*," on the regimental colour and appointments	—
——	Received the thanks of General Sir Ralph Abercromby, for its conduct in the action of Mandora	25
——	Furnished the guard at the head-quarters of the Commander-in-Chief	—

Year		Page
1801	*Battle of Alexandria* on the 21st of March	26
——	Death of General Sir Ralph Abercromby on 28th of March.	—
——	Marched to Aboukir, thence to *Rosetta*, and arrived before *Grand Cairo*.	—
——	Convention concluded at Cairo by which the place was surrendered, and the French troops were to be conveyed to France	—
——	The thanks of His Majesty, and of both Houses of Parliament, communicated to the army for the bravery evinced at the landing at Aboukir, and in the actions on the 13th and 21st of March	27
——	Promotion of Major Alexander Napier to be lieut.-colonel, in succession to Lieut.-Colonel Erskine, killed in action on the 13th of March	—
——	Letter from H. R. H. the Duke of York, Commander-in-Chief, announcing His Majesty's approval of the promotions taking place in the regiment in filling up the vacancies occasioned by the loss of Lieut.-Colonel Erskine	—
——	Regiment proceeded to Aboukir, and encamped before Alexandria	28
——	Alexandria surrendered by capitulation, and the campaign in Egypt terminated	—
——	The thanks of His Majesty, King George III., and of the two Houses of Parliament, communicated to the army employed in Egypt, and the Royal authority given for the *Sphinx* with the word "*Egypt*," to be borne on the regimental colours and appointments	—
——	The Grand Seignior conferred the order of Knighthood of the Crescent on the General	

Year		Page
	Officers, and presented gold medals to the officers employed with the army in Egypt: he also erected a palace at Constantinople for the future residence of the British Ambassadors	29
1801	List of the names of the officers of the NINETY-SECOND regiment, who received gold medals for service in Egypt.	—
——	Regiment marched for Aboukir and embarked for Malta, from whence it proceeded to Ireland	30
1802	The Peace of Amiens concluded . . .	—
——	Regiment embarked from Ireland, and proceeded to Glasgow	31
1803	War declared against France . . .	—
——	A second battalion added to the regiment formed from men raised under the *Army of Reserve Act*	—
——	Regiment removed from Glasgow to Weeley, where the second battalion was formed. .	—
——	Great preparations made in France for the invasion of England	32
1804	Napoleon Bonaparte created *Emperor of the French,* and *King of Italy* . . .	—
——	The *Additional Force Act* passed as a further measure of defence	—
——	The two battalions marched to Colchester, and encamped on Lexden Heath, from whence they returned to Weeley	33
——	Second battalion proceeded to Ireland . .	—
1805	First battalion brigaded with 42nd, 91st, and 95th (Rifle) regiments at Weeley. . .	—
——	Reviewed at Colchester by H.R.H. the Duke of York, the commander-in-chief . . .	—
——	Marched from Weeley to Ospringe and thence to Canterbury.	34

CONTENTS.

Year		Page
1806	Marched to London and attended the public funeral of Admiral Viscount Nelson at St. Paul's Cathedral	34
——	Major-General Honorable John Hope (afterwards Earl of Hopetoun) appointed to be colonel in succession to the Marquis of Huntly, removed to the 42nd regiment	—
1807	Embarked at Harwich on an expedition for Elsineur, under Lieut.-General Lord Cathcart, to take possession of the navy of Denmark .	35
——	Advanced to attack the Danes at Kioge with the troops under Major-General Sir Arthur Wellesley	36
——	Bombardment of Copenhagen, and surrender of the Danish fleet and stores to the British Government	37
——	General Orders expressing the approbation of His Majesty King George III., and of the Commander of the Forces, to the General and Staff Officers, and troops employed . .	38
——	Re-embarked for England and marched to Colchester	39
1808	Embarked at Harwich with an armament under Lieut.-General Sir John Moore and proceeded to Sweden	40
——	Returned to England and rendezvoused at Yarmouth, from whence the fleet proceeded to Spithead	—
——	Embarked for Portugal and joined the British army in that country	—
——	Proceeded with the force employed in Spain under Lieut.-General Sir John Moore . .	41
1809	Placed in position and bivouacked in front of Lugo	42

CONTENTS.

Year		Page
1809	Arrived at Corunna, and engaged in action with the French army	43
——	Lieut.-General Sir John Moore killed . .	—
——	Lieut.-Colonel Alexander Napier killed at the head of the NINETY-SECOND regiment, and Lieut.-Colonel John Lamont succeeded to the lieut.-colonelcy of the regiment . . .	—
——	Received the thanks of the two Houses of Parliament, and the Royal permission to bear the word "*Corunna*" on the regimental colour and appointments	44
——	Embarked at Corunna and disembarked at Portsmouth, from whence it marched to Weeley Barracks	—
——	Received orders to prepare again for foreign service	45
——	Embarked with the expedition under Lieut.-General the Earl of Chatham, for the Scheldt	—
——	The object of the expedition being thwarted, and much disease occurring among the troops, they re-embarked for England; the NINETY-SECOND regiment proceeded to Woodbridge . .	46
1810	Embarked a second time for the Peninsula, and joined the army under Lieut.-General the Viscount Wellington	47
1811	Marched from Lisbon and joined the army under Viscount Wellington in the lines of Torres Vedras	48
——	Brigaded with the 50th and 71st regiments .	49
——	Marshal Massena retreated from his position near Santarem, and pursued by the troops under Viscount Wellington	—
——	The siege of Badajoz commenced . . .	50

CONTENTS. xxxiii

Year		Page
1811	Regiment engaged at the Battle of *Fuentes d'Onor*	50
——	Received the Royal authority to bear the words "*Fuentes d'Onor*" on the regimental colour and appointments	51
——	The French retreated towards Ciudad Rodrigo, crossed the Agueda, and evacuated Almeida .	—
——	The siege of Badajoz raised . . .	52
——	*The battle of Albuhera.* . . .	—
——	The siege of Badajoz again commenced . .	—
——	The siege of Badajoz again relinquished . .	—
——	The British army recrossed the Guadiana . .	—
——	Marched to Elvas, and thence to Portalegre .	—
——	Investment of Ciudad Rodrigo . . .	—
——	Engagement at El Bodon . . .	—
——	Withdrew to Portalegre	—
——	Advanced towards Arroyo del Molinos . .	—
——	Attack and defeat of General Gerard's division at Arroyo del Molinos	54
——	The thanks of Lieut.-General Hill to the troops for their conduct in the action of Arroyo del Molinos	55
——	The approbation of H. R. H. the Prince Regent, and of H. R. H. the Commander-in-Chief, conveyed to the troops for their services in this action	—
——	Preparations made by Viscount Wellington for the recapture of *Ciudad Rodrigo* . .	56
——	The British troops entered Merida . .	—
1812	*Storm and capture of Ciudad Rodrigo* . .	57
——	Regiment marched to Albuquerque . .	—
——	Preparations made for the siege of Badajoz the *third* time	—
——	*Capture of Badajoz by assault* . . .	58

CONTENTS.

Year		Page
1812	Marched to the attack of Almaraz . . .	59
——	Destruction of the works and bridge at Almaraz	60
——	Received the Royal authority to bear the word "*Almaraz*" on the regimental colour and appointments	—
——	Marched to various stations preparatory to an attack on the forts of Salamanca. . .	61
——	*The Battle of Salamanca* . . .	62
——	The Marquis of Wellington entered Madrid .	63
——	Regiment moved to Aranjuez . . .	—
——	Siege of the castle of Burgos, which was afterwards raised	64
——	Defence of the town of Alba-de-Tormes . .	65
——	Marched into quarters at Coria . . .	66
1813	The French blew up the *Castle of Burgos*, and retreated	67
——	The French army took up a position in the neighbourhood of Vittoria	68
——	*The Battle of Vittoria*	—
——	The Royal authority was granted for the regiment to bear the word "*Vittoria*" on the regimental colour and appointments. . .	69
——	Skirmish at Almandoz.	70
——	Siege of St. Sebastian	—
——	Investment of Pampeluna by the Spaniards	—
——	Marshal Soult appointed to the command of the French army, with the title of *Lieutenant of the Emperor*	71
——	Regiment engaged at the Pass of Maya . .	—
——	Lieut.-Colonel Cameron permitted by His Majesty to bear the word *Maya* on his shield .	72
——	Number of officers and men killed and wounded in the action at Maya Pass . . .	— 73
——	Engaged at a village between Lizasso and Eguaros	74 —

CONTENTS. XXXV

Year		Page
1814	Again engaged on a height at Dona Maria	74
——	Received the Royal authority to bear the word "*Pyrenees*" on the regimental colour and appointments	75
——	Marched from Maya, and encamped near Roncesvalles	—
——	St. Sebastian and Pampeluna being taken, the British commander resolved to carry the war into France	—
——	Attack of the position on the *Nivelle*	76
——	Went into quarters at Cambo	—
——	Crossed the river *Nive*	77
——	Engaged in action at *St. Pierre*	—
——	Received the Royal authority to bear the word "*Nive*" on the regimental colour and appointments	78
——	Marched to St. Jean de Luz, and returned to Urt	79
——	Attacked and defeated the enemy at *Hellette*	—
——	Also at *Garris*	—
——	Affair at *Arriverete*	80
——	The Royal authority granted to Lieut.-Colonel Cameron, to bear on his crest the figure of a Highlander of the 92nd regiment, up to the middle in water, &c., &c., with the word *Arriverete*	—
——	Crossed the Gave d'Oleron, and moved on the road to *Orthes*	83
——	Engaged at the *battle of Orthes*	—
——	Received the Royal authority to bear the word "*Orthes*" on the regimental colour and appointments	—
——	Attack and defeat of the enemy at *Aire*	84
——	Orders issued to the troops engaged in the action at *aire*	85

Year		Page
1814	Address from the mayor and inhabitants of Aire	86
——	Regiment moved to Vic-Bigorre, in pursuit; thence to Tarbes and to Muret, on the road to Toulouse	87
——	The French evacuated *Toulouse*, the white flag was hoisted; and the British army entered the city.	88
——	Abdication of Napoleon announced	—
——	The intelligence disbelieved at *Bayonne*, from whence a desperate sortie was made by the French garrison	—
——	Regiment marched into Villa Franche, to Bezieze, and thence to Toulouse	89
——	Peace established between Great Britain and France: Louis XVIII. placed on the throne of France; and Napoleon Bonaparte proceeded to the Isle of Elba	—
——	Regiment marched to Blanchfort; thence to Pouillac	—
——	Received the Royal authority to bear the word "*Peninsula*," on the regimental colour and appointments	—
——	Moved down the Garonne in small craft, and embarked for Ireland	—
——	Disembarked at Monkstown, and marched to Fermoy	—
——	Received the thanks of Parliament for its meritorious and eminent services during the war	—
——	Inspected at Fermoy by Major-General Sir William Aylett, who testified his approbation of its appearance and interior economy	.
——	The second battalion disbanded at Edinburgh	90

CONTENTS. xxxvii

Year		Page
1815	Napoleon Bonaparte quitted Elba, and returned to Paris: Louis XVIII. withdrew to Ghent; and *Napoleon* resumed the dignity of *Emperor of the French*	—
——	Preparations for war immediately recommenced	—
——	Regiment embarked at Cork for Ostend; from thence proceeded to Bruges, and to Ghent	91
——	Marched to Brussels and brigaded . . .	—
——	Reviewed by Field-Marshal the Duke of Wellington	—
——	Action at Quatre-Bras	92
——	Colonel Cameron killed	—
——	Received the particular commendations of the Duke of Wellington	93
——	Number of officers and men killed and wounded at Quartre-Bas	—
——	*The Battle of Waterloo*	94
——	Destructive charge on a French column at *La Haye Sainte* by the Scots Greys and 92nd Regiment	96
——	The boldness and intrepidity of " *Les Braves Ecossais*" attracted the astonishment of Napoleon Bonaparte	—
——	The Prussian army on the road from Wavre .	—
——	The French made a last effort by a general attack, and were repulsed . . .	—
——	The allied troops advanced in pursuit, and forced the enemy to abandon every position, his artillery, arms, stores, &c. &c. . .	—
——	The victory at Waterloo thus was achieved, and a lasting peace has ensued . . .	97
——	Numbers of officers and men killed and wounded at *Waterloo*	—

Year		Page
1815	Honors and rewards conferred on the officers and men engaged in the battle of Waterloo .	97
——	Received the Royal authority to bear the word "*Waterloo*" on the regimental colour and appointments	—
——	The thanks of the Houses of Parliament communicated	98
——	Received also the thanks of the Highland Society of Scotland	—
——	The Allied army continued the pursuit of the French to Paris	—
——	General order issued by Field Marshal the Duke of Wellington, announcing that, in concert with Field-Marshal the Prince Blucher, he had concluded a military convention with the Commander-in-Chief of the French army near Paris, by which the French were to evacuate St. Denis, St. Ouen, Clichy, Neuilly, the heights of Monte Martre, and Paris, at specific and immediate periods; and congratulating the army upon the results of their glorious victory	—
——	Louis XVIII. returned to Paris, and was reinstated on the throne of France. . .	99
——	Napoleon Bonaparte fled to the South of France, and surrendered himself to the Captain of the British ship of war, the "Bellerophon." He was subsequently removed to the Island of St. Helena, which was agreed upon to be fixed as his future residence . . .	—
——	The British army was reviewed in camp near Paris by the Emperors of Austria and Russia, and other Sovereigns in alliance with Great Britain	—

CONTENTS.

Year		Page
1815	Regiment marched to St. Germains, and thence to Boulogne	99
——	Complimentary orders issued by Major-General Sir Denis Pack on the regiment quitting his command	—
——	Marched to Calais, and embarked for England	100
1816	Landed at Margate, and thence proceeded to Colchester, and subsequently to Edinburgh .	—
——	The Grand Duke Nicholas of Russia, while on a visit at Edinburgh, was present at an inspection of the regiment	—
1817	Embarked for Ireland	—
1819	Embarked for Jamaica	101
——	Sustained serious losses in officers and men from yellow fever	102
1820	Appointment of Lieut.-General John Hope to be Colonel in succession to General the Earl of Hopetoun, removed to the 42nd regiment	103
1823	Appointment of Lieut.-General Hon. Alexander Duff to be Colonel in succession to Lieut.-General Sir John Hope, removed to the 72nd Regiment	106
1824	Address from the magistrates and vestry of Trelawny on the good conduct of the regiment while stationed in that part of the island .	107
1825	The regiment formed into six *service*, and four *depôt* companies	109
1827	Embarked for England on being relieved by the 84th regiment	110
——	Landed at Portsmouth, and proceeded to Edinburgh castle	—
1828	Embarked for Ireland	111
1829	Lieut.-Colonel John McDonald, appointed from half-pay, assumed the command of the regiment	112

CONTENTS.

Year		Page
1830	Orders received for tartan trousers to be adopted on all occasions, when the kilt is not worn .	112
——	Inspected by Lieut.-General Sir John Byng, commanding the forces in Ireland, by whom great approbation was expressed on the state of the regiment	—
——	Address received from the magistrates of *Queen's County* on the good conduct of the regiment, particularly when called upon to aid the civil power	114
——	New colours presented to the regiment by Lieut.-General Sir John Byng, K.C.B., with a complimentary address	115
1831	Orders expressive of the approbation of the General Commanding in Chief of the conduct of the regiment, and of the zeal and exertions of Lieut.-Colonel McDonald . . .	118
——	Appointment of Lieut.-General Sir John Hamilton Dalrymple, Bart. (afterwards Earl of Stair) to be Colonel in succession to Lieut.-General Hon. Alexander Duff, removed to the 37th regiment	119
——	Inspected by Major-General Sir Edward Blakeney, K.C.B., by whom great commendation was bestowed	—
1832	Detachment employed in aid of the civil power, and in the protection of the magistrates .	120
1833	Regiment formed into six service and four depôt companies preparatory for foreign service	—
——	Depôt companies embarked for Scotland .	121
1834	Service companies embarked for Gibraltar .	—
1836	Ditto for Malta	—
——	Depôt companies embarked for Ireland . .	—
1837	Service companies inspected by Major-General Sir Henry Bouverie, K.C.B., commanding at Malta	—

CONTENTS.

Year		Page
1838	Inspected by H. R. H. Prince Maximilian of Bavaria, on his visit at Malta . . .	121
——	Furnished a Guard of Honor to receive Her Majesty the Queen Dowager, on her arrival at Malta	122
——	The Officers presented to Her Majesty . .	—
——	The Regiment passed in review before Her Majesty.	—
1840	Depôt companies embarked for Scotland	123
1841	Service companies embarked from Malta for the West Indies	—
1843	Appointment of Lieut.-General Sir William Macbean, K.C.B., to be Colonel in succession to General the Earl of Stair, removed to the 46th regiment	124
——	Service companies embarked from the West Indies for England	—
1844	Proceeded to Scotland, and joined by the depôt companies at Aberdeen	—
1846	Received the thanks of the Magistrates and Commissioners of Police at Edinburgh .	—
——	Embarked for Ireland	—
——	Colonel John McDonald promoted to the rank of Major-General, and Major John Alexander Forbes promoted to be Lieutenant-Colonel .	125
1850	Stationed in Ireland, and moved to Kilkenny .	—
——	Received orders to prepare for Foreign Service	—
——	Received complimentary address from the Mayor and Citizens of Kilkenny . . .	—
1851	Embarked for Corfu	—
——	THE CONCLUSION	126

PLATES.

Costume of the regiment . .	to face page	1
Colours of the regiment . .	,,	28
Plan of Arroyo-del-Molinos . .	,,	54
Two soldiers on duty . .	,,	126

d

SUCCESSION OF COLONELS

OF THE

NINETY-SECOND REGIMENT,

(HIGHLANDERS.)

Year		Page
1796	George, Marquis of Huntly, G.C.B.	127
1806	John, Earl of Hopetoun, G.C.B.	129
1820	Sir John Hope, G.C.B.	131
1823	Honorable Sir Alexander Duff, G.C.B.	132
1831	John, Earl of Stair, K.T.	—
1843	Sir William Macbean, K.C.B.	—

SUCCESSION OF LIEUTENANT-COLONELS . . 133

SUCCESSION OF MAJORS 134

APPENDIX.

	Page
General Order, dated 16th of May, 1801, relating to the campaign in Egypt, and the death of General Sir Ralph Abercromby	137
List of regiments, and names of the Commanding Officers, employed in Egypt in 1801	139
List of regiments employed in the expedition to Copenhagen in 1807	141
General Orders, dated 18th of January, and 1st of February, 1809, relating to the *Battle of Corunna*, and the death of Lieut.-General Sir John Moore, on the 16th of January, 1809.	142 & 144
List of regiments, and the names of the Commanding Officers, which composed the army under Lieut.-General Sir John Moore at Corunna	146
List of the British and Hanoverian regiments, as formed in brigades and divisions, and the names of the General Officers, and of the Commanding Officers of Regiments, at the *Battle of Waterloo*, on the 18th of June, 1815	147

HISTORICAL RECORD

OF

THE NINETY-SECOND REGIMENT,

(HIGHLANDERS.)

THE French Revolution, which commenced in the year 1789, by its destroying and sanguinary course, menaced Europe with universal anarchy. On the 21st of January, 1793, Louis XVI. was decapitated, and on the 1st of February the National Convention declared war against Great Britain and Holland. [1793]

Augmentations were in consequence made to the army; volunteer companies were formed by the patriotism of the British people, and every exertion was made to defend those institutions which had raised England to a high position among the nations of Europe.

To these events the NINETY-SECOND regiment owes its origin. A letter of service was addressed to the Duke of Gordon on the 10th of February, 1794, authorizing him to raise a regiment in Scotland, and the commission of Lieut.-Colonel Commandant was conferred upon his son the Marquis of Huntly. [1794]

The establishment of the regiment was directed to consist of one lieut.-colonel commandant, two majors,

1794 ten captains, one captain-lieutenant, twenty-one lieutenants, eight ensigns, one adjutant, quarter-master, surgeon, assistant-surgeon, chaplain, serjeant-major, quarter-master serjeant, forty serjeants, twenty drummers, two fifers, and one thousand rank and file.

On the 24th of June, 1794, the regiment was embodied at Aberdeen, and was generally known as "*The Gordon Highlanders*;" the regiment was inspected on the following day by Lieut.-General Sir Hector Munro, K.B., who expressed himself highly pleased with the general appearance of the corps.

The following officers were present, namely :—

Lieut.-Colonel Commandant . . George Marquis of Huntly.
Major . . . . Charles Erskine.

Captains.

Alexander Napier.
John Cameron.
Honorable John Ramsay.
Andrew Patton.
William McIntosh.
Alexander Gordon.
Simon McDonald.
John Gordon (*Capt.-Lieut.*)

Lieutenants.
Peter Grant.
Archibald McDonell.
Alexander Stewart.
John McLean.
Patrick Gordon.

Ensigns.
Charles Dowle.
George Davidson.
Archibald McDonald.
Alexander Fraser.
William Todd.
James Mitchell.

Adjutant . . John Henderson. | *Surgeon* . . William Findlay.
Quarter-Master . Peter Wilkie. | *Assistant Surgeon* John Clark.

Chaplain . . . . . William Gordon.

On the 9th of July, the regiment embarked at Fort George for England, and landed at Southampton on the 16th of August, when it was encamped on Netley Common. About this period it was numbered the *Hundredth* regiment.

The uniform of the officers was as follows:— 1794

JACKET.—Scarlet, facings yellow, with lappels turned back, and laced two and two; lace, silver, with a blue silk-worm in the centre; flat buttons, silver or plated, with the number of the regiment '100' in the centre.

EPAULETS.—Two for all ranks, of silver bullion, having two stripes of yellow silk in the centre of the strap, with a thistle, and a binding of blue round the edge.

WAISTCOAT.—Scarlet, with regimental buttons, and laced with silver.

BELTED PLAID.—Twelve yards of blue, black, and green tartan, with a narrow yellow stripe.

PURSE, SHOES, AND HOSE.—Badger skin, ornamented with six white tassels, mounted with silver, and having a rim of silver round the top. The shoes were low-quartered, with silver buckles. The rosettes and garters were of red tape. The hose were tartan of white and red chequer.

The sword was the Highland claymore; the sword belt of buff leather, and the breastplate oval, of silver, ornamented with a crown and thistle, encircled by the words "*Gordon Highlanders.*"

The sash was of crimson silk, and was worn across the left shoulder. The bonnet was ornamented with black ostrich feathers, and the dirk was silver mounted.

The dress of the serjeants and privates was similar, the arms of the former being the claymore and halbert, and the latter had muskets; queues were worn by officers and men.

On the 5th of September, the regiment embarked at Southampton for Gibraltar, where it landed on the 27th of October: at this station the drill of the regiment was completed, and it was immediately placed

1794 on the garrison roster. The effective strength consisted of three field officers, seven captains, nine lieutenants, six ensigns, four staff, twenty-nine serjeants, twenty-one drummers, and seven hundred and twenty-seven rank and file.

In December the regiment received its colours on Windmill Hill, after being consecrated by the garrison chaplain; the regiment was marched under them by files in ordinary time, previously to which the Marquis of Huntly made a very impressive address, calling the attention of the officers and men to the duties which their King and Country expected from them, and to the honors which he trusted they would acquire under these banners.

The first or King's Colour was, as usual, the Great Union. The second, or Regimental Colour, was composed of yellow silk; in the centre of both, the number '100,' surmounted with a crown, and the words "*Gordon Highlanders*," the whole within a wreath of thistles and roses.

1795 On the 11th of June, 1795, the regiment embarked for Corsica, and landed at Bastia on the 11th of July.

In February of the previous year a landing was effected in Corsica by the allied troops, and, through the influence of General Paoli, the Commander-in-Chief of the island, a decree was made by the Assembly of Deputies, declaring the separation of Corsica from France, and its union to the British dominions.

In December, 1795, Lieut.-Colonel the Marquis of Huntly obtained leave of absence, and the command of the regiment devolved on Major Erskine.

1796 The regiment was inspected on the 14th of April, 1796, at Bastia, by Lieut.-General Thomas Trigge, commanding at Corsica, who expressed his gratification at the appearance of the men, and the very correct 1796 manner in which they performed the different movements.

On the 14th of May, His Excellency the Viceroy, Lieut.-General Sir Gilbert Eliott reviewed the regiment, and signified his highest approbation of its appearance.

On the following day, the greater portion of the regiment, under the command of Major Alexander Napier, to which rank he had been promoted in March of this year, proceeded to *Corte*, in order to suppress a serious rebellion which broke out in that part of the island, and upon the return of the troops, a general order was issued by Lieut.-General the Honorable John Thomas De Burgh, who had succeeded to the command of the forces in Corsica, expressive of his best thanks for the exertions and good conduct displayed during the above fatiguing service.

Lieut.-Colonel Commandant the Marquis of Huntly was promoted to the rank of colonel of the regiment on the 3rd of May, 1796; Major Charles Erskine was also promoted to the rank of Lieut.-Colonel, the commission of the latter being ante-dated 1st May of the previous year.

In July Lieut.-Colonel Erskine obtained leave of absence, and the command of the regiment devolved upon Major Napier.

On the 14th of August, a detachment, consisting of one field officer, two captains, four subalterns, seven serjeants, eight corporals, and two hundred privates, was ordered to be held in readiness at a moment's notice, to embark upon a secret expedition. The zeal and spirit of the corps showed itself in a most conspicuous manner, by the unanimous wish of the whole

1796 to be employed upon it; and in consequence of which, Major Napier, then commanding the regiment, made an offer to that effect to the Commander-in-Chief, who was pleased to give the following answer :—

"The Commander-in-Chief is sensible of the zeal "and laudable motive, which have induced the officers "and men of the Hundredth regiment to offer their "services on the present occasion, and he desires Major "Napier to express his best thanks to them, as well "as his assurance, that he will be ready at all times to "testify his satisfaction at their general good conduct "and appearance, although circumstances will not at "this time allow him to avail himself of their services "to the extent they offer them."

This expedition proved to be against *Porto Ferrajo*, in the Isle of Elba, and was completely successful, without any loss on the part of the troops employed.

Meanwhile the brilliant career of General Bonaparte in Italy had produced a change of sentiment among the inhabitants of Corsica, of which island he was a native. The Corsicans, therefore, gloried in him as a man who reflected honor on their country, and they regretted that the island had been annexed to Great Britain, as this event placed them in hostility to their victorious countryman, and they began to concert measures to effect its separation. It appearing evident that the expense of the defence would exceed the advantage derived from the possession of the island, the British troops were withdrawn, and on the 6th of September the regiment embarked for Gibraltar.

The regiment mustered one major, five captains, seven lieutenants, five ensigns, three staff, thirty-seven serjeants, twenty-one drummers, and seven hundred and six rank and file.

The following General Order was issued upon this occasion:—

5th September, 1796.

"The Hundredth regiment being to embark for "Gibraltar, Lieut.-General De Burgh cannot suffer "them to leave Corsica, without testifying his appro- "bation and satisfaction of their general good conduct "and soldier-like behaviour, since he had the honor to "command them; at the same time he desires they "will accept of his best wishes for their success and "welfare on all occasions."

During the voyage, the British Admiral fell in with a large fleet of Spanish men-of-war, and the first intimation he had of Spain being at war with Great Britain, was their firing upon his ships. Perceiving this, and the enemy being so superior in force, he made signal to crowd all sail. The Spaniards, however, captured the "Granby" transport, having on board two staff officers, three serjeants, and forty-eight rank and file of the regiment.

The regiment landed at Gibraltar on the 4th of October, and on the 10th of that month was inspected by the Lieut.-Governor, who was much pleased with its appearance.

In the previous year, Prussia had concluded a peace with the French Republic, and in consequence of the United Provinces of Holland having leagued with France, England had taken possession of the Cape of Good Hope and of Ceylon. The former allies of England now became converted into enemies. War was declared by Holland, which had been constituted the Batavian Republic, against Great Britain, in May, and Spain followed the example in October. In the same month, Lord Malmsbury was sent to Paris to

1796 negociate a peace on the part of the British Government; but the French insisted upon retaining, as integral parts of the Republic, the conquests lately made; these terms could not be acceded to consistently with the general interests of Europe, and the negociation was discontinued.

1797 In April, 1797, Lieut.-Colonel Erskine arrived at Gibraltar, and assumed the command of the regiment.

In April, the preliminaries of peace were signed at Leoben, in Styria, between Austria and the French Republic, so that Great Britain was left to continue the contest single-handed with France and her allies. In July Lord Malmsbury was sent a second time to negociate a peace, but the demands of the French Directory rendered the attempt abortive. On the 17th of October the definitive treaty of peace between Austria and the French Republic was signed at Campo Formio.

1798 The regiment embarked in transports for England on the 16th of March, 1798. The ships put into the Tagus on the 9th of April, and sailed again on the 15th. After a tedious and boisterous passage, the regiment disembarked at Portsmouth on the 15th of May, and occupied Hilsea Barracks.

The effective strength of the regiment at this period consisted of two field officers, four captains, eleven subalterns, three staff, thirty-seven serjeants, twenty-two drummers, and seven hundred and forty-two rank and file.

By a General Order, dated 26th of May, 1798, it was directed that the coats of the army should be worn buttoned over the body down to the waist.

On the 31st of May, the regiment embarked in ships of war at Southsea Beach, Portsmouth, for Ireland,

and arrived at Dublin, on the 15th of June, where it went into barracks. 1798

His Majesty King George III., appointed Colonel the Marquis of Huntly to serve as a Brigadier-General upon the Staff of the Army in Ireland, in which country a spirit of discontent had been fomented by a party of unprincipled men, who had expected aid from France to carry out their designs. On the 21st of June, Lieut.-General Lake defeated the main body of the rebels at Vinegar-hill, and the troubles in Ireland would have subsided, had it not been for the expected aid to be derived from France.

On the 2nd of July, the regiment marched at a moment's notice, in consequence of the disturbed state of the country, the urgency of the service being such that the troops were conveyed in carriages.

The regiment encamped in the vicinity of Gorey on the 7th of July, and on the 18th marched suddenly to Blessington, where it encamped. On the 29th it marched and encamped at the Glen of Emall.

On the 10th of August, Lieut.-Colonel Erskine and three hunded men were detached and encamped at Torbay.

The following letter, expressive of the good conduct of the regiment during their stay at Gorey, was addressed by the Dean of Ferns, to Colonel the Marquis of Huntly:—

"MY LORD,
"I have the honor of enclosing to you that part
" of the proceedings in the last vestry, held in Gorey,
" wherein your Lordship and your regiment are
" mentioned. This mark of our respect and gratitude
" should have been sooner expressed and conveyed to

1798 " you, had not our calamitous situation delayed the
" calling of a vestry, which we conceived the most regu-
" lar mode of expressing our sentiments collectively.

" It may be pleasing to your Lordship to hear that,
" in the attendance of my parish, I have heard all the
" poor loud in the praise of the honesty and humanity
" of the privates of your regiment. They not only did
" not rob them of the wretched pittance that was left
" by the rebels, but refused such trifling presents (of
" provisions, &c.,) as were offered them, saying their
" King paid them nobly, and enabled them to supply
" every want at their own expense.

" I have the honor to be,
" With great respect,
" Your Lordship's obedient Servant,
(Signed) " PETER BROWN,
" *Dean of Ferns.*"

" We the loyal inhabitants of the parish and vicinity
" of Gorey, in vestry assembled, beg leave thus publicly
" to acknowledge the goodness and humanity evinced
" by the Marquis of Huntly, during his short stay
" amongst us. We are proud to add, that during that
" short stay, rapine ceased to be a system, and the
" confidence of the people in the honor of government
" began to revive. We should be wanting in grati-
" tude if we omitted our testimony, that the humanity
" of the colonel was emulated by the soldiers, and we
" request the Hundredth regiment to accept our thanks
" for the moderation and honor which marked the
" conduct of every individual officer and private who
" composed it.

(Signed) " PETER BROWN, *Rector.*
" J. JERMAN, *Churchwarden.*"

The French, to the number of about nine hundred 1798 men, commanded by General Humbert, landed at Killala, and being joined by a few malcontents marched to Castlebar.

On the 24th of August the regiment marched to Blessington; on the 26th encamped at Kilbeggan; on the 28th at Athlone; on the 29th at Ballymore, in a position in front of the town; on the 1st of September it encamped at Crophill, and moved every day until the 16th, when it encamped near Moat.

Meanwhile the united French and rebel force had been attacked by Lieut.-General Lake, at Ballinamuck, on the 8th of September, and the French troops were compelled to surrender at discretion.

Major-General John Moore, in brigade orders, dated 25th of September, 1798, after detailing some irregularity on the part of the troops, added—

" The Major-General must, in justice to the Hun-
" dredth regiment, state, that hitherto he has had no
" complaint of any one of them, nor has he ever met
" them in town after the retreat beating."

The thanks of both Houses of Parliament were, on the 15th of October, conveyed to the troops, " for their
" meritorious exertions on the present important
" crisis."

While the regiment was encamped near Moat, the following order was received, by which the corps was numbered the NINETY-SECOND regiment.*

---

* The ninety-first, ninety-second, ninety-third, ninety-fourth, ninety-fifth, ninety-sixth, ninety-seventh, and ninety-ninth regiments, which were directed to be raised at the commencement of the war with France in 1793, were afterwards disbanded, so that the *ninety-eighth* was numbered the *ninety-first*, and the *Hundredth* became the NINETY-SECOND regiment.

1798 *Adjutant-General's Office, Dublin, 16th October, 1798.*

"It is His Majesty's pleasure, that the "Hundredth regiment shall in future be numbered the "NINETY-SECOND, and that it be placed on the same "establishment with regard to field officers as other "regiments of the line."

(Signed)   G. HEWITT, *Adjutant-General.*

On the 30th of October, 1798, the regiment broke up from camp, and went into quarters at Athlone.

Napoleon Bonaparte, against whose legions in Egypt and the Peninsula, the NINETY-SECOND regiment, in subsequent years, acquired great renown, was now rising, step by step, to that imperial sway which he afterwards attained. The National Convention had been succeeded in October, 1795, by the French Directory, and the latter, jealous of Bonaparte's popularity, sent him, in May, 1798, on the expedition to Egypt. Napoleon took Alexandria by storm, and soon established himself at Cairo. The Sublime Porte, incensed by the invasion of Egypt, declared war against France, and formed an alliance with Russia. The fleet which had conveyed the expedition to Egypt, was almost destroyed by Admiral Nelson in Aboukir Bay, on the 1st of August. So large a portion of the French army, being thus secluded in a distant land, gave fresh impulse to the allies, and in November the island of Minorca surrendered to the British arms. In December, 1798, the co-operation of Russia against France was secured by Great Britain.

1799 War was declared by the French Directory against Austria, in March, 1799, and the combined Austrian and Russian armies recovered the greater portion of Italy.

Great Britain now determined to make a corre- 1799
sponding attempt, in conjunction with Russia, to recover
Holland from the dominion of France, and a numerous
army was selected to proceed to that country under
His Royal Highness the Duke of York, previous to
whose arrival, the troops were to be commanded by
Lieut.-General Sir Ralph Abercromby.

A plan of co-operation was concerted between Great
Britain and Russia, in the expectation that the Dutch
would rise in arms against the French, in favour of the
Prince of Orange, and, aided by the Anglo-Russian
force, would exert themselves to effect their emancipation.

On the 15th of June, the NINETY-SECOND regiment,
which had been selected to embark on the expedition
to Holland, commenced its march by divisions for
Cork, on which day the following address was received
by the commanding officer:—

" At a numerous meeting of the inhabitants of Athlone
" and its vicinity on the 15th June, 1799, Thomas Mit-
" chell, Esq., in the chair: the following Address to
" Lieut.-Colonel Erskine, commanding His Majesty's
" NINETY-SECOND regiment in this garrison, was unani-
" mously agreed to:—

" SIR,
    " We heard with concern, that His Majesty's
" NINETY-SECOND regiment, which you have com-
" manded in this garrison, has been ordered to march
" for the purpose of joining those troops intended for
" a foreign expedition; but however we may regret
" your departure, we are not surprised that a regiment,
" so eminently conspicuous for its steadiness and dis-
" cipline, should be selected for an arduous enterprise.

1799 " We have during your continuance amongst us,
" experienced a polite attention from the officers of
" your regiment, and the uninterrupted peace and
" tranquillity, which have prevailed in this town and
" neighbourhood, evince the attention of the soldiers
" under your command.

" Permit us, therefore, to return you our thanks, and
" to request that you will convey the same to the
" officers, non-commissioned officers, and soldiers of
" your regiment.

" By order of the meeting,
(Signed) " THOMAS MITCHELL."

The regiment arrived at Cork on the 24th and 25th of June, and encamped at Monkstown, until orders for its embarkation should arrive. On the 19th of July, the regiment embarked at Cove, and arrived at Dover on the 30th, when it encamped on Barham Downs, where the troops were assembling for the expedition to Holland under the orders of Lieut.-General Sir Ralph Abercromby.

The NINETY-SECOND regiment was placed in the fourth brigade, commanded by Major-General, afterwards Sir John Moore, which consisted of the Royals (second battalion), twenty-fifth, forty-ninth, seventy-ninth, and NINETY-SECOND regiments.

The regiment marched for Ramsgate on the 7th of August, and on the following day embarked in transports, which sailed on the 11th for the coast of Holland. Its effective strength consisted of one colonel, one lieut.-colonel, two majors, six captains, twelve lieutenants, seven ensigns, five staff, forty serjeants, twenty-one drummers, and seven hundred and thirty rank and file.

The British troops landed on the Dutch coast, near 1799 the *Helder*, on the 27th of August. A considerable body of French and Dutch troops assembled near the point of debarkation; some sharp fighting occurred, and in the evening the enemy retreated to a position six miles in his rear. Although one of the first to get a footing on the Dutch shores, it did not fall to the lot of the NINETY-SECOND to be materially engaged this day in the affairs on the sand-hills. The regiment had one serjeant and fourteen rank and file drowned in the landing on the Dutch coast. The enemy having abandoned his fortifications, and evacuated the town during the night, the regiment moved into Helder on the 28th of August. A numerous train of heavy and field artillery was found in this important post; two days afterwards the Dutch fleet surrendered without striking a blow, and hoisted the colours of the Prince of Orange.

On the 1st of September, the regiment marched out of Helder, and on the 2nd advanced to Oude Sluys, on the Zuyder Zee, where the army took up a position, along which the troops were placed in cantonments, the NINETY-SECOND being in advance of the right.

The Dutch did not manifest a disposition to rise against the French. At daylight, in the morning of the 10th of September, the united French and Dutch forces, under General Brune, attacked the piquets; the troops repaired to their alarm-posts, and the action soon became general: the British troops repulsed the attack, and the orders of that day directed the regiment to its cantonments at Oude Sluys, and conveyed the thanks of General Sir Ralph Abercromby* for its "noble and steady conduct during the "day."

Captain the Honorable John Ramsay was wounded in this action, which was fought near the villages of *Crabbendam* and *Schagen*.

Field-Marshal His Royal Highness the Duke of York arrived at the Helder on the 14th of September, and, having been reinforced by a corps of twelve thousand Russians, under Lieut.-General Hermann, resolved on attacking the French position in advance of *Alkmaar*, reaching from Zuyder Zee, on the right, to Camperdown on the left, and embracing the town of Bergen. The attack was made on the 19th of September, in four columns, but the Russians having failed in holding Bergen, after having entered it in gallant style, the places, which had been acquired by the other columns, were abandoned, and His Royal Highness withdrew his army to its former position on the Zuype.

From the 20th of September until the 1st of October both armies remained within their entrenchments, strengthening their lines of defence: the French had received reinforcements, and had inundated a large tract of country on their right by cutting the sluices, thus contracting the ground of operations to six or seven miles.

The Duke of York, on the 2nd of October, made another attempt on the French position, between Bergen and *Egmont-op-Zee*. The combined attacks were made in four columns: the division under General Sir Ralph Abercromby being on the right, marched

---

* Lieut.-General Sir Ralph Abercromby, K.B., was promoted to the local rank of General on the Continent of Europe, on the 13th of August 1799.

along the beach. The left of the French army was 1799 posted and concentrated about Bergen, a large village surrounded by extensive woods, through which passed the great road leading to Haarlem; between which and the sea was an extensive region of high sand-hills, impassable for artillery. Behind the sand-hills, and to the enemy's right, through the whole extent of North Holland, lies a wet and low country, intersected with dykes, canals, and ditches.

The army advanced before daylight to attack the enemy. The NINETY-SECOND regiment was ordered to escort twenty pieces of artillery to the front, along the sea-shore. In the performance of this duty it was attacked by a column of nearly six thousand men at *Egmont-op-Zee*, where a most sanguinary conflict ensued, immediately under the eye of General Sir Ralph Abercromby.

Trusting to their superior numbers the French advanced with resolution, and fairly met the bayonets of the regiment, now commanded by Lieut.-Colonel Erskine, Colonel the Marquis of Huntly having been wounded in the charge, which completely overthrew the enemy, and preserved the guns.*

---

* Colonel the Marquis of Huntly commanded the regiment in this memorable charge, which began and decided the action at Egmont-op-Zee: all the rest was a pursuit. The Marquis of Huntly, and Major-General (afterwards Sir John) Moore, were wounded, and the command of the regiment devolved upon Lieut.-Colonel Erskine.

Major-General Moore was carried to the surgeon by two soldiers of the regiment; and a few years afterwards, when writing for a drawing of the uniform, for the purpose of having a soldier of the NINETY-SECOND as one of the supporters to his coat of arms, on being made a Knight of the Bath, he mentioned the circumstance of their having remarked—" There is the General, we must take him to the " doctor;" and then added, " We can do no more; we must join the " lads, for every man is wanted ! !" Major-General Moore, on his

1799 The French centre was supported by the town of *Alkmaar*, and General Sir Ralph Abercromby had passed Bergen in order to turn the French position at Alkmaar, to which place the NINETY-SECOND, immediately after the brilliant affair, before recorded, advanced. As the men fought hand-to-hand, the conflict was signalized by many feats of individual bravery and devoted courage.

The action was maintained with great obstinacy on both sides until night, when the enemy retired, leaving the British masters of the field of battle.

In the despatch of His Royal Highness the Duke of York, dated Zuyper Sluys, 4th of October, it was stated that, " the points where this well-fought battle were " principally contested, were from the sea-shore in " front of Egmont, extending along the sandy desert, " or hills, to the heights above Bergen, and it was sus- " tained by the British columns, under those highly " distinguished officers, General Sir Ralph Aber- " cromby, and Lieut.-General Dundas, whose exertions, " as well as the gallantry of the brave troops they led, " cannot have been surpassed by any former instance of " British valour."

The NINETY-SECOND had Captain William McIntosh, Lieutenants George Fraser, Gordon McCardy, and

---

recovery, inquired for these men in order to reward them, and offered twenty pounds, but no one claimed it; and he remarked, that " it was a noble trait of the regiment, that no men in its ranks came " forward to personate the parties, or to claim the reward."—It was, therefore, supposed they were killed.

It may be observed, that this is one of the few instances on record of *crossing bayonets* by large bodies. Even the supernumerary rank of the NINETY-SECOND on this occasion was bayoneted; among the number Lieutenant McCardy was killed, and Lieutenant Donald McDonald (who afterwards succeeded to the command of the regiment at Waterloo) received three bayonet wounds.

sixty-five rank and file killed; Colonel the Marquis of Huntly, Captains John Cameron, Alexander Gordon, John McLean, and Peter Grant, Lieutenants Norman McLeod, Charles Chad, Donald McDonald, Charles Cameron, and John McPherson, Ensigns George William Holmes, James Bent, and two hundred and eight rank and file wounded.

1799

The gallant conduct evinced by the NINETY-SECOND on this occasion was afterwards rewarded with the Royal authority to bear the word *Egmont-op-Zee* on the regimental colour and appointments.

His Royal Highness the Commander-in-Chief, in the General Order of the 5th of October, at Alkmaar, expressed "his warmest thanks for the steady perse-
" vering gallantry of their conduct in the general action
" of the 2nd instant, and to which he ascribes the
" complete victory gained over the enemy;" and, with the rest of the army, the regiment received the thanks of both Houses of Parliament.

The regiment, commanded by Lieut.-Colonel Erskine, subsequently shared in the general operations of the army, but was not engaged in any very serious affair.

The gallant exertions made on behalf of the Dutch were not seconded by them; and in the meantime the French army had been reinforced. Instead, therefore, of fighting for a people who were not resolved to be free, it was decided that the British troops should be withdrawn from Holland. A convention was ultimately concluded with General Brune at Alkmaar on the 18th of October, and on the following day a cessation of hostilities was proclaimed.

The regiment marched on the 28th of October to Colenzugby, near the Helder, embarked the same day

1799 on board of His Majesty's ships "Kent" and "Monarch," and landed at Yarmouth on the day following. Its effective strength consisted of twenty-four serjeants, twenty drummers, and four hundred and forty-six rank and file.

During the campaign from the 27th of August to the 28th of October, the regiment sustained a loss of three officers and ninety-three rank and file, several of the wounded soldiers having died.

On the 4th of November the regiment marched *en route* to Chelmsford, where it arrived on the 10th, and was placed in the eighth brigade, the command of which Major-General Moore assumed on the 25th of December 1799.

Here the regiment received canvas knapsacks, painted yellow, having a circle of red in the centre, in which the Crown and Thistle, with the words "*Gordon Highlanders*," were inserted.

1800 Napoleon Bonaparte having returned from Egypt to Paris in the previous year, had been appointed First Consul of France, and made overtures for peace; but the British Ministry, considering that the French government had not acquired sufficient stability, showed no desire to accede to the proposal.

On the 10th of April, 1800, orders were issued for the regiment to hold itself in readiness to march at the shortest notice; the first division marched on the 12th, and was followed by the others on the 14th and 15th, for the Isle of Wight, where it arrived on the 23rd of April.

The regiment, under the command of Lieut.-Colonel Erskine, marched for Cowes on the 27th of May, and embarked on the same day in vessels of war. The head-quarters, and five companies in His Majesty's ship

"Diadem," sailed on the 30th. The officers and men 1800 present with the regiment consisted of one lieut.-colonel, two majors, seven captains, sixteen lieutenants, six ensigns, six staff, thirty-six serjeants, twenty-two drummers, and six hundred rank and file.

The regiment disembarked at the Isle de Houat, on the coast of France, on the 7th of June, where it encamped, under the command of Brigadier-General the Honorable Thomas Maitland.

On the 18th of June, the NINETY-SECOND regiment embarked on board His Majesty's ship "Terrible," destined with others to make an attack on Belle-Isle, but which was abandoned; on the 20th the regiment disembarked, and occupied its former encampment on the Isle de Houat.

The NINETY-SECOND embarked on the 23rd of June, with other regiments for the Mediterranean, under the command of Colonel the Earl of Dalhousie, of the Second, or the Queen's Royals, in His Majesty's ship "Diadem," and arrived at Port Mahon, in the Island of Minorca, on the 20th of July.

General Sir Ralph Abercromby, K.B., arrived at Minorca on the 4th of August, and took the command of the troops there assembled. The regiment disembarked on the 7th, and was inspected, on the 11th of August, by Sir Ralph Abercromby.

The NINETY-SECOND regiment embarked at George's Town on the 30th of August, and sailed on the following day. After touching at Gibraltar, it proceeded to *Cadiz*, arrived in the bay on the 3rd of October,—and made preparations to land. The enemy, however, sent a flag of truce, but a disease was ravaging the city at the time, and the fleet quitted the coast in order to avoid

1800 infection, proceeding afterwards to Gibraltar, where it arrived on the 29th of October.

The regiment arrived at Minorca on the 6th of November, sailed again on the 21st, and anchored at Malta on the 1st of December. This island, after a blockade of two years, had been compelled by famine, to surrender in September, 1800, to Great Britain.

The British Government having resolved to effect the expulsion of the French from Egypt, an army* amounting to about fifteen thousand men, of which the NINETY-SECOND formed part, was assembled under General Sir Ralph Abercromby, at Marmorice Bay, on the coast of Asiatic Turkey. The regiment sailed from Malta on the 26th of December, and arrived at Marmorice Bay on the 29th. During the foregoing period, the regiment was occasionally landed for exercise and practice, as if before an enemy.

1801 Some weeks were lost at Marmorice, in expectation of receiving reinforcements of Greeks and Turks; and the expedition did not proceed to its final destination until the 23rd of February, 1801. On the 2nd of March, it anchored in the Bay of Aboukir, eastward of Alexandria; but notwithstanding all the exertions of the navy, under Admiral Lord Keith's orders, the necessary arrangements could not be made for landing the troops, until a week afterwards, in consequence of unfavorable weather, and other obstructions.

A landing was effected on the 8th of March; a body of French troops, supported by several batteries, awaited the arrival of their opponents, but were forced to give way in defiance of every exertion, and after severe loss on both sides.

---

* List of regiments which served in Egypt in 1801, is inserted in the Appendix, page 133.

The NINETY-SECOND, under the command of Lieut.- 1801
Colonel Erskine, landed during the action, and took up a position for the night on the heights of Aboukir. The regiment mustered one lieut.-colonel, two majors, six captains, ten lieutenants, six ensigns, six staff, fifty serjeants, twenty-two drummers, and six hundred and seventy-two rank and file.

On the 9th of March, the regiment advanced about a mile further towards *Alexandria*. On the day following, it marched to the heights of *Mandora*, and remained in position, while the artillery and stores were being landed. Nothing of importance occurred this day, beyond a smart skirmish, as the enemy slowly retired.

The army again moved forward on the 12th of March, and came in sight of the enemy, who was strongly posted with his right to the canal of *Alexandria*, and his left to the sea.

About six o'clock in the morning of the 13th of March, the British army advanced to attack the enemy's position on the heights in front of *Mandora*, the NINETY-SECOND being directed to lead the left column into action. The enemy having opened a most destructive fire from his artillery, enfiladed the column to its whole depth: orders were consequently given to deploy into line. The enemy thought this a favorable moment, and immediately advanced to the attack. The NINETY-SECOND, being in advance of the line, was exposed to a very galling fire of grape-shot, and at the same time was attacked by the 61st Demi-Brigade; the regiment, however, continued unshaken in its advance to the very muzzles of the guns, and succeeded in taking two field-pieces, and one howitzer, completely routing the enemy who defended them, and possessing itself of the right of his position. He was forced, there-

1801 fore, to retire to the fortified heights of Nicopolis, under the walls of Alexandria, to which they form the principal defence from that side.

Lieut.-Colonel, afterwards General Sir Robert Thomas Wilson, in his History of the British Expedition to Egypt, stated that—

"The British had not advanced out of the wood of "date trees, which was in front of Mandora Tower, "before the enemy left the heights on which they had "been formed, and moved down by their right, com- "mencing a heavy fire of musketry, and from all their "cannon, on the NINETY-SECOND regiment, which formed "the advanced guard of the left column." After eulogising the gallantry of the ninetieth regiment, which formed the advanced guard of the right column, Lieut.-Colonel Wilson, added :—

"The conduct of the NINETY-SECOND had been no "less meritorious. Opposed to a tremendous fire, and "suffering severely from the French line, they never "receded a foot, but maintained the contest alone, "until the marines and the rest of the line came to "their support."

The gallantry and good conduct of the regiment this day were most conspicuous, and in commemoration thereof, the NINETY-SECOND afterwards received the Royal Authority to bear the word "*Mandora*" on the regimental colour and appointments.

His Majesty's service, and the NINETY-SECOND regiment in particular, sustained a great loss in the death of Lieut.-Colonel Charles Erskine, who was mortally wounded early in the action, when the command of the regiment devolved on Major Alexander Napier.

The following officers were wounded: Captains Hon. John Ramsay and Archibald McDonell; Lieutenants,

Norman McLeod, Charles Dowle (mortally), Donald McDonald, Tomlin Campbell (mortally), Alexander Clarke (mortally), and Ronald Macdonald; Ensigns, Peter Wilkie and Alexander Cameron; twenty-two rank and file were killed, and seventy-seven were wounded.

On the 14th of March, the army occupied the position, from which the enemy was driven the day before, and the troops were employed in throwing up works. On this day, General Sir Ralph Abercromby thanked the troops for their soldier-like and intrepid conduct, in the action of yesterday, and particularised the NINETY-SECOND regiment. It may not be irrelevant to state, that he selected the regiment to furnish the guard at his head-quarters from his first landing in Egypt, to the hour of his death; and the regiment was continued by Lieut.-General (afterwards Lord) Hutchinson, on that duty, until its final departure from that country.

In consequence of the reduced state of the regiment from sickness, and the casualties of the 13th of March, it was ordered on the 20th of March (with the exception of the Commander-in-Chief's Guard), to march at three o'clock next morning to relieve the battalion of marines at Aboukir Castle; where the following Brigade Order was issued :—

" Major-General Coote feels extreme concern, that
" the NINETY-SECOND regiment is ordered to march to
" Aboukir; he hopes they will soon return to the army,
" and cannot part with that corps without requesting,
" that the officers and men will accept his best thanks,
" for their attention to their duty since they have been
" under his command."

About half an hour after the regiment commenced

1801 its march on the 21st of March for Aboukir, when the French forces at *Alexandria*, having been augmented by the arrival of additional troops from the interior, advanced under General Menou, to attack the British position. Major Alexander Napier, upon hearing the firing, immediately countermarched the regiment, and resumed his former station in the line, in which it was hotly engaged throughout the day: no sooner had the enemy retired from this struggle, and resigned the victory to the British army, than the army became aware of the loss it had sustained in the Commander-in-Chief, General Sir Ralph Abercromby, who received a mortal wound at the commencement of the action, but which he concealed until the battle was decided. Sir Ralph Abercromby died on the 28th of March, and was buried at Malta.

The NINETY-SECOND had Captain John Cameron, and Lieutenant James Stewart Mathison wounded; three rank and file killed; and forty-four wounded.

Orders were again issued for the march of the regiment on the following morning, provided no attack was made by the enemy, and it accordingly marched to *Aboukir*.

On the 2nd of May, the regiment marched from Aboukir for *Rosetta*, where a Turkish force joined the British; on the 5th it advanced along the banks of the Nile, and continued in motion until the 16th of June, when it arrived before *Grand-Cairo*.

The regiment moved to the right on the 21st of June, and encamped before the town of *Gizeh*; one of the gates of which place was delivered up by the French on the 28th of June.

A convention with the garrison of *Cairo*, was on the following day announced as finally adjusted, by which that place was to be delivered up to the allied army, and the French troops to be transported to France.

On the 14th of July, Lieut.-General Hutchinson communicated to the army the thanks of His Majesty, and of both Houses of Parliament, for its determined bravery at the landing, and in the actions of the 13th, and 21st of March, and concluded by a warm eulogium from himself.

The army marched, and retraced its steps towards *Rosetta*. The promotion of Major Alexander Napier to the Lieutenant-Colonelcy, in succession to Lieut.-Colonel Erskine, killed in the action of the 13th of March, was announced in a manner most flattering to the corps on the 15th of July, as will appear from the following extract of a letter from His Royal Highness the Duke of York, the Commander-in-Chief, dated—

"Horse Guards, 30th May, 1801.
" My Lord,

" I need not assure you how sincerely I unite with
" you in regretting the loss of so deserving an officer
" as Lieutenant-Colonel Erskine, of the NINETY-SECOND
" regiment. I have ever entertained too high a sense
" of the gallant services of that corps, not to have re-
" commended upon this occasion, that the succession
" should go in the regiment, of which His Majesty has
" been pleased to approve.

" I am, &c.
(Signed) " FREDERICK,
" *Commander-in-Chief.*
" *Major-General The Marquis of Huntly."*

The regiment arrived on the heights of *Aboukir* on the 8th of August, and on the following day marched

1801 to the same position which it had left on the 22nd of March, and encamped before Alexandria.

The brigade under the orders of Brigadier-General John Doyle, Colonel of the eighty-seventh regiment, advanced before daylight on the 17th of August to attack two redoubts, situated on the green-hill in front of the enemy's right, which the thirtieth and fiftieth regiments were directed against, while the NINETY-SECOND was placed as a reserve, and ready to support either. This service was successfully performed with little loss to the regiment.

Troops having been sent in boats on the 26th of August to land, and break ground to the westward of *Alexandria*, the enemy this day sent out a flag of truce, and hostilities ceased; on the 2nd of September, Alexandria surrendered by capitulation, which event terminated the campaign in Egypt.

The British troops received the thanks of both Houses of Parliament, and His Majesty King George III., conferred upon the NINETY-SECOND, and other regiments, which had thus exalted the military fame of Great Britain, by the expulsion of the " invincible" legions of Bonaparte from Egypt, from whence he had expected to extend his conquests throughout Asia, the honor of bearing on their colours and appointments the " SPHINX," and the word " EGYPT," as a distinguished mark of His Majesty's royal approbation of their conduct during the campaign.*

The Grand Seignior established the Order of Knighthood of the Crescent, of which the General Officers were made members; and large gold medals

---

* *Vide* General Order, dated Horse Guards, 16th of May, 1801, and List of regiments employed in Egypt, inserted in pages 131, &c. of the Appendix.

92ND REGIMENT (GORDON HIGHLANDERS.)

For Cannon's Military Records

were presented to the field officers, captains, and subalterns. As a further proof of the estimation in which the Grand Seignior held the services of the British soldiers in Egypt, he ordered a palace to be built at Constantinople, for the future residence of the British Ambassadors.

1801

Names of the officers of the NINETY-SECOND regiment, who received gold medals for service in Egypt.

Lieutenant-Colonel . . . . Alexander Napier.
Major . . . . John Gordon.

Captains.

John Cameron.
The Hon. John Ramsay.
Andrew Patten.

Archibald McDonell.
Peter Grant.
Patrick Gordon.

Lieutenants.

Norman McLeod.
Charles Dowle.
Donald McDonald.
John Forman.
James Lee.
George W. Holmes.

James Bent.
Ronald Macdonald.
James Stewart Mathison.
Charles Straubenzie.
William Phipps.

Ensigns.

Peter Wilkie.
William Mackay.
Alexander Anderson.

Charles Duddingstone.
Alexander Cameron.
William Logie.

Paymaster . Archibald Campbell.
Adjutant . Dugald Campbell.
QuarterMaster Peter Wilkie.

Surgeon . Archibald Hamilton.
Assist.-Surgeons. { Wm. Cook.
J. R. Hume.

The regiment marched for Aboukir on the 6th of October, 1801, and embarked in ships of war, which sailed on the following day.

Upon the guard of the NINETY-SECOND, which had been doing duty at head-quarters, being ordered to rejoin, the officer commanding the regiment received a

1801 letter expressive of Lieut.-General Hutchinson's "entire
" approbation of the exemplary conduct of the guard,
" and of Serjeant Mark in particular."

On the 19th of October, the regiment arrived at Malta, and remained in harbour until the 15th of November, when the ships sailed for the shores of Great Britain.

1802 The regiment arrived at Cork on the 30th of January, 1802, and remained under quarantine at Cove, until the 12th of February, when it landed and marched to Kilkenny. The effective strength consisted of one lieut.-colonel, two majors, four captains, fifteen lieutenants, five ensigns, six staff, forty-two serjeants, twenty-two drummers, and five hundred and fifty-nine rank and file.

On the 27th of March, 1802, a definitive treaty of peace was signed at Amiens between the French Republic, Spain, and the Batavian Republic, on the one part, and Great Britain on the other. The principal features of the treaty were, that Great Britain restored all her conquests during the war, excepting Trinidad and Ceylon, which were ceded to her, the former by Spain, and the latter by the Batavian Republic. Portugal was maintained in its integrity, excepting that some of its possessions in Guiana were ceded to France. The territories of the Ottoman Porte were likewise maintained in their integrity. The Ionian Republic was recognised, and Malta was to be restored to the Knights of St. John of Jerusalem. The French agreed to evacuate the Neapolitan and Roman States, and Great Britain all the ports that she held in the Adriatic and the Mediterranean.

The regiment on the 5th of April received orders to fire a *feu-de-joie*, in consequence of the treaty of peace concluded at Amiens. On the 12th of April, the regiment marched from Kilkenny, and arrived at Belfast on the 28th of that month, where it remained until the 2nd of June, when it embarked for Scotland. 1802

On the 4th of June, the regiment arrived in Scotland for the first time since it was raised, and proceeded to Glasgow.

The peace of Amiens was of short duration; it inspired no confidence of ultimate tranquillity, and both parties remained prepared to renew the contest. The chief complaint on the part of France was the non-evacuation of Malta by the British troops, and the asylum afforded to the enemies of the French government. Circumstances had, however, occurred which would have rendered the restoration of Malta to the Knights of St. John of Jerusalem equivalent to ceding that island to France. Other grounds of irritation existed, and the designs of Napoleon Bonaparte to raise the power of France by an extension of territorial dominion, to which England appeared a barrier, caused the struggle to be renewed; and the contest was not settled until the final defeat of the French at the battle of Waterloo, on the memorable 18th of June, 1815, by the allied troops under the Duke of Wellington. 1803

On the 18th of May, 1803, war was declared against France; Hanover was overrun by the French, and severed for a time from the British crown; and the First Consul ordered the arrest of all British subjects in the territories of the French and Batavian republics.

Preparations were made by the British Government to meet the emergency; the "*Army of Reserve Act*" was passed in June, 1803, for raising men for home service by ballot, by which a second battalion was added to the NINETY-SECOND regiment. The second

1803 battalion was to be composed from the balloted men raised in Scotland for limited service, and was placed on the Establishment from the 9th of July following.

In June, the regiment was removed from Glasgow to Colchester, and on the 1st of July it marched to Weeley, where it encamped while the barracks were being prepared, which were occupied by the regiment during the winter.

The second battalion of the regiment was formed at Weeley, on the 24th of November, 1803; officers and non-commissioned officers, with a proportion of old soldiers, being posted to it from the first battalion for the purpose of instruction. Both battalions were commanded by Lieut.-Colonel Napier.

Each battalion was to have ten companies, consisting of fifty-four serjeants, twenty drummers, two fifers, and a thousand rank and file.

At this period Bonaparte was making preparations for the invasion of England, for which purpose he collected an immense flotilla at Boulogne. The threat of invasion aroused the patriotism of the British people, and the most strenuous measures were pursued to defeat the designs of the French Ruler; volunteer and yeomanry corps were formed in every part of the kingdom, and all parties united in one grand effort for the preservation of Great Britain.

1804 In May, 1804, Napoleon was invested with the dignity of *Emperor of the French,* and on the 26th of May, of the following year, he was crowned at Milan as *King of Italy*.

Further measures of defence were adopted by Great Britain, and the " *Additional Force Act*" was passed on the 14th July, 1804.

Both battalions marched to Colchester on the 24th of July, and on the 6th of August were encamped on Lexden Heath.

On the 24th of October orders were issued for the march of one captain, one subaltern, four serjeants, four corporals, and one drummer to Elgin, from the second battalion, to receive the men to be raised under the "*Additional Force Act.*"

Both battalions broke up from Lexden camp on the 26th of October, and marched to Weeley barracks.

Orders were received on the 25th of November for the second battalion to be held in readiness to march from Weeley barracks, and proceed by the inland navigation to Liverpool, from whence it was to embark for Ireland. The second battalion accordingly marched in three divisions, on the 29th of November and on the two following days.

The first battalion, under the command of Lieut.-Colonel Napier, remained in Weeley barracks during the winter.

During the summer of 1805, the first battalion was brigaded with the forty-second, ninety-first, and ninety-fifth (Rifle) regiments. On the 2nd of September, the battalion marched from Weeley to Colchester; on the 4th of September the first battalion was ordered to hold itself in readiness for embarkation, but on the 6th of September it returned to Weeley barracks.

The first battalion marched, on the 7th of October, to Colchester with other troops, and was reviewed by His Royal Highness the Duke of York, the Commander-in-Chief, who expressed himself particularly pleased with the appearance of the battalion, which returned to its quarters at Weeley on the 18th of October.

1805 While the French were pursuing their victorious career in Germany, they experienced great reverses from the British navy. On the 21st of October, the combined fleets of France and Spain were defeated off Cape Trafalgar; but the victory was purchased with the loss of Admiral Viscount Nelson, whose remains were honored with a public funeral at St. Paul's Cathedral, and the first battalion of the NINETY-SECOND regiment attended the ceremony.

On the 29th of October, the first battalion marched from Weeley, and arrived at Ospringe barracks on the 6th of November; on the 26th of November it marched to Canterbury.

1806 The first battalion marched, on the 2nd of January, 1806, to London, to attend the public funeral of Admiral Viscount Nelson, whose remains were interred, on the 9th of January, in St. Paul's Cathedral, where a monument was erected by authority of Parliament at the public expense.

Major-General the Hon. John Hope, from the sixtieth regiment, (afterwards the Earl of Hopetoun,) was appointed by His Majesty King George III. to be colonel of the NINETY-SECOND regiment, on the 3rd of January, 1806, in succession to Major-General the Marquis of Huntly, who was removed to the forty-second, or the Royal Highlanders, on the decease of General Sir Hector Munro, K.B.

The first battalion marched, on the 11th of January, from London for Colchester, where it arrived on the 15th of that month: it marched to Weeley barracks on the 29th of May, where it remained stationary, with the exception of occasional marches to and from Colchester, for the purpose of being exercised with other brigades.

On the 3rd of February, 1807, the first battalion marched from Weeley for Harwich, with the view of checking the infection of ophthalmia, which then prevailed among the troops at Weeley. The first battalion returned to Weeley on the 27th of April.

Information having been obtained that Napoleon purposed employing the navy of *Denmark* against Great Britain, an armament was prepared for obtaining possession of the Danish fleet by treaty or force, on the assurance that it should be restored at the conclusion of the war with France. The first battalion was destined to share in this enterprise, and it received orders, on the 22nd of July, to be in readiness for foreign service.

The battalion, commanded by Lieut.-Colonel Napier, marched for Harwich on the 26th of July, and embarked on the same day, after being inspected by Lieut.-General Sir David Baird. On the 27th a draft of one hundred and three rank and file joined from the second battalion: the effective strength of the first battalion consisted of forty-eight serjeants, nineteen drummers, and nine hundred and eighty-one rank and file.

On the 1st of August, the expedition sailed, and on the 8th anchored in the Sound near Elsineur. On the following day, Lieut.-General Harry Burrard* directed the army assembling in the Sound to be formed in brigades and divisions, and that the forty-third, fifty-second, NINETY-SECOND, and ninety-fifth (Rifle) regiments should compose the reserve, under Major-General Sir Arthur Wellesley, until the arrival of the Commander-in-Chief.

Lieut.-General Lord Cathcart arrived on the 12th of

---

* Lieut.-General Burrard was created a Baronet in November 1807.

1807 August, and assumed the command of the army; on the 14th the fleet sailed towards *Copenhagen*, and on the 16th of August the army landed at Vedeck, in Zealand, situated about half-way between Elsineur and Copenhagen, without opposition, and on the following day the regiment went into cantonments in Hassan, and Broomskoy. Its movements were various, and dependent upon circumstances during this period.

The NINETY-SECOND regiment advanced towards Roeskelde on the 26th of August, in consequence of the enemy collecting a large force at the town of *Kioge* and its vicinity, for the purpose of being thrown into *Copenhagen*, which was at this time invested by the British army.

On the 29th of August, the division under Major-General Sir Arthur Wellesley advanced to attack the Danes in their position. The NINETY-SECOND regiment, under the command of Lieut.-Colonel Alexander Napier, was appointed to lead the infantry against the enemy's camp, in which the regiment charged him, driving him out of it, and through the town of Kioge, with the loss of his artillery. The regiment had two rank and file killed, and one wounded.

On the 30th of August, the British troops marched to Osted, and went into cantonments. On this day, after expressing in orders his satisfaction at the conduct of the troops in the action of the 29th, Major-General Sir Arthur Wellesley, in particularizing those who had an opportunity of distinguishing themselves, alluded to the conduct of the NINETY-SECOND regiment, and of *Lieut.-Colonel Napier*, in the attack of the enemy in his camp, and to the regular and orderly manner in which the troops marched through Kioge, and formed beyond the town.

The conduct of the troops employed in the action 1807 before *Kioge* was thus alluded to in General Orders by Lieut.-General Lord Cathcart:—

" Head Quarters, Hellerup,
1st September, 1807.

" The Commander of the Forces desires to express, in
" the strongest manner, his thanks to Major-General
" Sir Arthur Wellesley, and to the officers and men of
" the division under his command, for the judgment,
" valour, and discipline exhibited in the two attacks
" made upon the enemy in the general action of the
" 29th of August at Kioge.

" The details of this affair, as reported by the Major-
" General, will be laid before His Majesty by the
" earliest opportunity."

The bombardment of Copenhagen induced the Crown Prince to listen to terms; and on the 7th of September the Danish fleet and stores were surrendered to the British government on condition of being restored, when a general pacification should take place.

The following General Order was issued to the troops on the same day :—

" 7th September, 1807.

" The Commander of the Forces congratulates the
" army on the capitulation of Copenhagen, which
" includes the surrender of the Danish fleet."

A detachment of grenadiers took possession of the citadel, and hostilities ceased.

The object of the expedition having been accomplished, Copenhagen was evacuated, and the NINETY-SECOND regiment marched from Osted to Roeskelde Kroe on the 23rd of September, and on the next day joined the army before Copenhagen, and went into cantonments.

1807

The approbation of His Majesty, King George III., for the services performed during the expedition, was expressed in the following extract from a despatch, dated 16th September, 1807, addressed to Lieut.-General Lord Cathcart by Viscount Castlereagh, Principal Secretary of State for the War Department:—

"His Majesty has received, with great satisfaction, "the account of the particular services rendered in their "detached commands by Major-General the Right "Hon. Sir Arthur Wellesley, Major-General Von "Linsingen, and Brigadier-General Von Decken.

"I am further to express His Royal pleasure, that "you do convey to the general officers under your "command His Majesty's full approbation of the zeal, "ability, and valour they have displayed in their "several departments; and your Lordship will make "it known to the army, that the conduct of all his "troops, both British and Hanoverian, who have so "much distinguished themselves by their valour and "good conduct, is highly acceptable to His Majesty.*

"It is also a matter highly pleasing to His Majesty, "that through the whole of this expedition, such a "perfect harmony, and such a zealous spirit of co-ope-"ration, have pervaded all departments of the naval "and military service."

Lieut.-General Lord Cathcart, in communicating the above to the army under his command, on the 28th of September, 1807, added,—

"The Commander of the Forces cannot make this "communication, without renewing his thanks to the "army, for the assistance he has received from the

---

* A list of the regiments employed in the expedition to *Copenhagen* is inserted in the Appendix, page 135.

"zeal, advice, and active services of the generals, staff, 1807 "and commanding officers, and for the patience, dis- "cipline, and exertions of all regiments, corps, and "departments, to which, under the blessing of Provi- "dence, he is indebted for the complete success of "the expedition, and for the most gracious approba- "tion, which His Majesty has been pleased to declare "of the whole service."

On the 17th of October, the first battalion of the NINETY-SECOND regiment embarked for England in the *Minotaur*, *Neptunis*, and *Iris*, ships of war, and sailed on the 21st. During the passage they encountered very boisterous weather, in which the ships parted company: unfortunately the *Neptunis*, of ninety-eight guns (one of the captured Danish ships), with six hundred of the NINETY-SECOND regiment on board, got aground, and was totally lost. The men were landed on the island of Hewan, where they remained for fourteen days, until vessels arrived for them from England.

The men on board the head-quarter ship landed in England on the 12th of November; and on the arrival of the different detachments, orders were waiting for them to proceed to Weeley barracks. The effective strength of the first battalion at this period consisted of forty-nine serjeants, twenty-two drummers, and nine hundred and sixty-four rank and file.

The first battalion marched to Colchester barracks 1808 on the 23rd of March, 1808. Volunteers from the militia of the northern counties were, about this time, received, and taken on the strength of the second bat- talion, which continued in Ireland.

On the 19th of April, the first battalion of the regi- ment was directed to be held in readiness for immediate

1808 embarkation for foreign service, and on the 29th of April, it marched from Colchester, and embarked in transports at Harwich, under Lieut.-Colonel Napier.

The battalion sailed for Yarmouth on the 4th of May, and arrived there on the 6th, where an armament, under the command of Lieut.-General Sir John Moore, was assembling, destined to proceed to Sweden.

The armament sailed from Yarmouth on the 10th of May, and anchored off *Gottenburg* on the 17th. The Swedes did not show any inclination to avail themselves of British assistance on shore, consequently the troops did not disembark, but during their stay were occasionally exercised in practising to land from launches and flat-bottomed boats.

The fleet sailed for England on the 3rd of July, with orders to rendezvous at Yarmouth. A vessel, with orders from England, however, changed the place of rendezvous to the Downs, where the fleet arrived on the 20th of July, and proceeded to Spithead. A draft of seventy rank and file was received from the second battalion.

Spain was at this period the centre of political interest. Portugal, deserted by her government, and Spain betrayed, the people of each rose in arms to recover the national independence. Dissensions had arisen in the royal family of Spain, occasioned by the sway of Emanuel Godoy, who bore the title of Prince of Peace. This minister was dismissed, but the Court was unable to restore tranquillity. In this emergency, the French Emperor was solicited to be umpire; and Napoleon ultimately seized the crown of Spain, which he placed on the head of his brother Joseph, who was transferred from the throne of Naples. Europe was indignant, and Spain furious, at this usurpation. The

Spaniards flew to arms, and the British government 1808 resolved to aid the Spanish and Portuguese patriots; a British army accordingly proceeded to the Peninsula in June, 1808, the command of which was held by Lieut.-General Sir Arthur Wellesley.

On the 31st of July, having received on board a fresh supply of provisions and water, the first battalion sailed for Portugal, and on the 19th of August arrived in Mondego Bay. Marshal Junot and the French army having been defeated by the troops under Lieut.-General Sir Arthur Wellesley, in the battles at *Roliça* on the 17th, and *Vimiera* on the 21st of August, sued for a cessation of hostilities.

The battalion landed at Maciera Bay on the 27th of August, and the convention of Cintra was signed on the 30th of that month, by which it was stipulated that the French should evacuate Portugal.

Portugal, being thus rescued from the presence of hostile troops, orders arrived from England for Lieut.-General Sir John Moore to take the chief command of a part of the army, which was to be employed in Spain; with a notification that a force from England, under the command of Lieut.-General Sir David Baird, was to land at Corunna, and co-operate with him. The first battalion of the NINETY-SECOND regiment was immediately put in motion towards the frontiers, and arrived at Portalegre on the 11th of October, 1808.

On the 26th of October, the first battalion, being placed in the division commanded by Lieut.-General Sir John Hope, moved from Portalegre, and on the 2nd of November entered Spain, at Badajoz; marching by Merida, Truxillo, and Talavera, it arrived at the Escurial on the 22nd of November, and halted.

The enemy having pressed forward to Valladolid

1808 and Tordesillas, thereby threatening to cut off Lieut.-General Sir John Hope's communication with the army under Lieut.-General Sir John Moore, who was then at Salamanca, the battalion marched from the Escurial, on the 27th of November, across the Guadarama mountains, and moving by Villa Castin and Avila, it arrived at Alva de Tormes on the 4th of December.

The battalion advanced from Alva de Tormes towards Tordesillas, on the 11th of December, and Lieut.-General Sir John Moore, learning that the French were moving upon him from the direction of Madrid, which had by this time surrendered, while another column was advancing from the direction of Burgos, moved to the left, to form a junction with Lieut.-General Sir David Baird, crossed the Douro at Toro, and arrived at Vallada on the 21st of December. On the 24th of that month, the battalion marched by Benevente, Astorga, and Villa Franca, arriving at Lugo on the 4th of January, 1809.

1809 The troops took up a position in front of Lugo, on the 6th of January, 1809, and remained bivouacked, in order of battle, until the 8th, when they marched in the night, and arrived at *Corunna* on the 11th. During these marches, in common with the rest of the army, the battalion suffered from fatigue and the severity of the weather.

On the 12th of January, the battalion was placed in position in front of *Corunna;* and on the 14th and 15th the women, sick men, and baggage, were embarked for England.

The British army having accomplished one of the most celebrated retreats recorded in modern history, repulsing the pursuing enemy in all his attacks, and having traversed two hundred and fifty miles of mountainous country under very disheartening circumstances, accompanied by severe privation, was not destined to embark for England without a battle.

Marshal Soult, Duke of Dalmatia, having taken up a position above the town of *Corunna*, made arrangements for attacking the British army as soon as the troops should commence their embarkation. The sick men, women, and baggage having been conveyed on board ship, preparations were made for embarking the troops on the 16th of January, 1809. The French instantly descended from the heights in three columns, and advanced about two o'clock to attack the British position in front of *Corunna*; a sanguinary action ensued, and before dark, the French were defeated in all their attacks. Lieut.-General Sir John Moore was killed; and the battle was scarcely ended, when, wrapped in a military cloak, his remains were interred in the citadel of Corunna, over which Marshal Soult, with the true feeling of a soldier, erected a monument.

This victory enabled the British troops to be embarked without further molestation. In this battle the first battalion of the NINETY-SECOND was posted towards the left of the army, on the road leading to Betanzas, and throughout the day supported its former reputation.

The NINETY-SECOND, together with the rest of the army, had not only to lament the death of Lieut.-General Sir John Moore, but also that of their own commanding-officer, Lieut.-Colonel Alexander Napier, who was killed at its head: the command therefore devolved on Brevet Lieut.-Colonel John Lamont, who was afterwards promoted lieut.-colonel in the regiment. Lieutenant Archibald McDonald was severely wounded

1809 on this occasion, and died shortly afterwards. Only two rank and file of the battalion were killed, and four wounded.

This army received the thanks of both Houses of Parliament, "for its distinguished discipline, firmness, and valour, in the battle of CORUNNA," which were communicated to the regiment, with the following letter, addressed to the commanding-officer by Lieut.-General Sir David Baird :—

"SIR, *Portsmouth, 30th January,* 1809.

" In communicating to you this most signal
" mark of the approbation of the Parliament of the
" United Kingdom of Great Britain and Ireland, allow
" me to add my warmest congratulations upon a dis-
" tinction, which you, and the corps under your com-
" mand on that day, had a share in obtaining for His
" Majesty's service.

" I have, &c.,
(Signed) " DAVID BAIRD, *Lieut.-General.*
Officer commanding First Battalion,
NINETY-SECOND *regiment.*"

The conduct of the battalion during the expedition, and its gallantry at the battle of Corunna, were rewarded by the Royal authority for the word "CORUNNA" to be borne on the regimental colour and appointments of the NINETY-SECOND, in common with the army employed under Lieut.-General Sir John Moore.*

On the 17th of January, the battalion embarked at Corunna, and on the 26th disembarked at Portsmouth, marching immediately for Weeley Barracks, where the

---

* Vide General Orders of the 18th of January and 1st of February, 1809 ; also a list of regiments employed under Lieut.-General Sir John Moore at Corunna, inserted in pages 136, &c., of the Appendix.

several divisions arrived on the 13th, 14th, and 15th 1809 of February.

On the 16th of February, orders were issued that every exertion should be made to clothe and equip the the regiment again for foreign service. The regiment received black painted canvas knapsacks, having the Sphinx and number on the back.

About this period, Lieut.-Colonel John Cameron joined from the second battalion, which continued in Ireland.

The first battalion marched on the 29th of June for Dover, where it arrived on the 6th and 7th of July, and was joined by two hundred and twenty rank and file from the second battalion.

During the summer of 1809 great preparations were made by the British Government for fitting out the most formidable armament that had, for a long time, issued from England. It consisted of an army of forty thousand men, commanded by Lieut.-General the Earl of Chatham, and of thirty-nine ships of the line, thirty-six frigates, and numerous gun-boats, bomb-vessels, with other small craft, under Admiral Sir Richard Strachan. The object of the expedition was to gain possession of the islands at the mouth of the Scheldt, and to destroy the French ships in that river, with the docks and arsenals at Antwerp.

On the 14th of July, the first battalion marched to Deal, and embarked in ships of war with other troops there assembled, under Lieut.-General the Earl of Chatham. The battalion, under the command of Lieut.-Colonel Cameron, was placed in Major-General Sir William Erskine's brigade, and in the division commanded by Lieut.-General Sir John Hope. The NINETY-SECOND mustered forty-four serjeants, twenty

1809 drummers, and nine hundred and seventy-four rank and file.

The expedition sailed from the Downs on the 28th of July, and landed on the 1st of August on the Island of South Beveland, near Goes, and went into cantonments in that place and Capelle. Flushing surrendered on the 15th of August; but during the siege Marshal Bernadotte had arrived at Antwerp, put the place in a posture of defence, and removed the ships higher up the river. In consequence of these preparations, the reduction of Antwerp was deemed impracticable by a Council of War, and on the 1st of September the NINETY-SECOND embarked for England.

The battalion landed at Landguard Fort near Harwich, and proceeded to Woodbridge barracks. During the time it was in South Beveland, it suffered much from fever and ague, with other diseases peculiar to that place; consequently every attention was now paid to restore the men, and to render them again fit for service.

1810 On the 11th of July, 1810, the first battalion of the NINETY-SECOND embarked at Landguard Fort, landed at Ramsgate, and arrived at Canterbury on the 20th of that month.

The battalion was shortly afterwards destined to proceed a second time to the Peninsula, and it embarked from Deal for Lisbon on the 24th of September. Since its embarkation at Corunna, in January, 1809, great events had occurred in Spain, and the French had obtained possession of Corunna, Bilboa, and all the important places on the northern coast of that country. Saragossa, after a gallant defence, had also fallen, and Marshal Soult having overrun Gallicia, marched into the northern provinces of Portugal, and obtained possession of Oporto. The small British force which had been left in Portugal, when Lieut.-General Sir John Moore advanced into Spain, was concentrated by Lieut.-General Sir John Cradock for the defence of Lisbon.

1810

The British Government resolved to make another effort to save Portugal from invasion, and also to assist the Spaniards in their struggle for independence. Accordingly in April, 1809, Lieut.-General Sir Arthur Wellesley was sent with reinforcements to Portugal, and was appointed to the command of the British army in the Peninsula. His first object was to dislodge Marshal Soult from Oporto. The famous passage of the Douro led to the fall of Oporto, and the French Marshal was compelled to retreat. The Spanish General Cuesta having been defeated, with great loss, by the division of the French army under Marshal Victor, Lieut.-General Sir Arthur Wellesley was obliged to desist from the pursuit of Marshal Soult.

In the beginning of July, the British army advanced into Spain, and a junction being effected with General Cuesta, the combined forces occupied a strong position at *Talavera*. Here they were attacked on the 27th and 28th of July, 1809, and the French army, commanded by Joseph Bonaparte in person, was defeated; for which victory Lieut.-General Sir Arthur Wellesley was raised to the peerage by the title of *Viscount Wellington*.

After this victory it was deemed necessary to make a retrograde movement on Badajoz, information having been received that Marshals Soult, Ney, and Victor had united their forces, and were advancing to fall on the rear of the allied army.

Viscount Wellington now became occupied with the

1810 defence of Portugal. The French armies in Spain had been reinforced during the winter of 1809-10 with troops from Germany, peace having been concluded between France and Austria; and in April, 1810, the Emperor Napoleon espoused the Archduchess Maria Louisa, daughter of the Emperor of Austria.

Spain having been reduced to French domination, Napoleon resolved to subjugate Portugal, and Marshal Massena, Prince of Essling, assumed the command of the "*Army of Portugal*" in May. Ciudad Rodrigo and Almeida were captured by the French, who were, however, gallantly repulsed at the *Sierra de Busaco* on the 27th of September, 1810, after which Viscount Wellington occupied the strong position of Torres Vedras, about thirty miles from Lisbon.

This was the state of affairs in the Peninsula when the NINETY-SECOND arrived in the Tagus. On the 8th of October, the battalion landed, and the necessary camp equipage, on taking the field, was immediately issued.

1811 The NINETY-SECOND, under the command of Lieut.-Colonel John Cameron, marched from Lisbon to join the army under Viscount Wellington, then in the fortified lines of Torres Vedras, and arrived at Cruzandera on the 15th of October, where the battalion remained until the 15th of November. At this period it was attached to the first division of the army, and was brigaded with the *fiftieth* and *seventy-first* regiments, under Major-General Howard.

Marshal Massena having abandoned his position in front of the British, and retired upon Santarem, the NINETY-SECOND advanced on the 15th of November, and occupied the village of Almostal on the 19th of November, moving on the 28th to Alcantrinha, the enemy occupying a strong position at Santarem, immediately in front of the British army. 1811.

At the commencement of the year 1811, Lisbon was the point on which the interests of the British nation in foreign affairs were concentrated, and the question whether Portugal should remain independent, or become subject to France, was to be decided by the two great armies posted near Lisbon, the one for attack, the other for defence.

The difficulty of supplying his troops with necessaries in a devastated country, and the impracticability of forcing the fortified lines of Viscount Wellington, at Torres Vedras, at length compelled Marshal Massena to consult the safety of his army by a seasonable retreat.

During the night of the 5th of March, the enemy broke up from his position near Santarem, and retreated in the direction of Almeida. Viscount Wellington immediately pursued Marshal Massena by Thomar, Pombal, Redinha, and Espinhal, at each of which places some sharp affairs took place, honorable to the British arms, as well as at Sabugal on the 3rd of April, immediately after which the French continued their retreat into Spain.

The first battalion of the NINETY-SECOND regiment entered Spain on the 9th of April, and was cantoned in Albergaria, where a detachment of one lieutenant and forty-four rank and file joined from the second battalion, then in Ireland. At this period, the sixth division of the British army invested *Almeida,* and a force of British and Portuguese under Marshal Beresford was employed in the Alemtejo and Spanish Estremadura, which compelled the enemy to abandon Campo Mayor. *Olivenza* was next besieged by Mar-

1811 shal Beresford, and retaken on the 15th of April, after which he broke ground before *Badajoz*.

Marshal Massena had reached Ciudad Rodrigo on the 25th of April, and, having concentrated his forces, crossed the Agueda on the 2nd of May, and advanced towards the allied army, posted between that river and the Coa, in order to relieve *Almeida*. On the approach of the French, the British light division and cavalry fell back upon *Fuentes d'Onor*, where three other divisions were posted, and in which Viscount Wellington determined to receive the attack of the enemy.

The village of *Fuentes d'Onor* is situated on low ground, at the bottom of a ravine, with an old chapel and some buildings on a craggy eminence which overhang one end. In the afternoon of the 3rd of May, the enemy attacked the village with a very large force, and was repulsed with loss. On this occasion, the light company of the NINETY-SECOND distinguished itself. Lieutenant James Hill was wounded; nine rank and file were likewise wounded.

The main body of the British army was concentrated in the vicinity of Fuentes d'Onor in the course of the evening and following day. On the 5th of May, the enemy, very superior to the British in numbers, made an attack on the right of the allied position early in the morning, and also on the village, which he repeated during the day, and the action became general. Each of his attacks was successively repulsed, and towards the evening, the victory being decidedly in favour of the British, the French retired to their original position.

On this occasion, the first battalion of the NINETY-SECOND regiment, commanded by Lieut.-Colonel Cameron, was stationed to the right of *Fuentes d'Onor*, covering a brigade of nine-pounders, and was exposed 1811 to a very heavy cannonade. The light company, and a subdivision of each of the others in its front, were warmly engaged throughout the day, and eminently distinguished themselves. Major Archibald McDonnell, who commanded them, was in consequence promoted to the brevet rank of Lieut.-Colonel. Major Peter Grant and Lieutenant Allan McNab were severely wounded; the latter died two days afterwards. The battalion had also seven rank and file killed and thirty-five wounded.

The NINETY-SECOND afterwards received the Royal Authority to bear the words "FUENTES D'ONOR" on the regimental colour and appointments, in commemoration of the gallantry displayed by the first battalion in that battle.

Both armies continued in their positions during the 6th and 7th of May without any particular occurrence, and on the morning of the 8th, the rear of the enemy's columns was seen retreating on the road towards Ciudad Rodrigo. The NINETY-SECOND still remained bivouacked near Fuentes d'Onor.

The French crossed the Agueda and left *Almeida* to its fate. That place was evacuated by General Brennier at midnight of the 10th of May, when the enemy blew up the works, and the greater part of the garrison succeeded in effecting its escape during the night.

On the 14th of May, the battalion returned to its former cantonments in Albergaria, where orders were received increasing its establishment to twelve hundred rank and file.

Marshal Beresford, in the meantime, was continuing the blockade of *Badajoz*; but receiving information

1811 that Marshal Soult was advancing from Seville to its relief, he raised the siege on the 15th of May, and having concentrated his force, marched to meet the enemy. On the following day, the battle of *Albuhera* was fought, and the British gained a brilliant but hard-earned victory. In the night of the 17th, Marshal Soult left Badajoz to its fate, and commenced his retreat towards Seville.

Viscount Wellington now gave orders for *Badajoz* to be again closely invested. To assist in these operations, the brigade, of which the NINETY-SECOND formed part, was appointed the first in the second division of the army, under Lieut.-General Rowland (afterwards Viscount) Hill, at this time in Spanish Estremadura, covering the siege of Badajoz.

The battalion, under Lieut.-Colonel Cameron, marched, on the 25th of May, from Albergaria for the Alemtejo, crossed the Tagus at Villa Velha, and the Guadiana above Badajoz, and joined the second division in front of Albuhera, on the 10th of June, about ten days after the second siege of Badajoz had been commenced. Its effective strength consisted of fifty-six serjeants, sixteen drummers, and eight hundred and twenty-five rank and file.

Marshal Marmont, with the French army of Portugal, having effected a junction with that of the south, under Marshal Soult, they advanced to relieve Badajoz; Viscount Wellington found it therefore necessary to relinquish the siege, and to withdraw the allied army across the Guadiana.

Accordingly, the second division, on the 16th of June, broke up from its bivouac in front of Albuhera, marched by Valverde, recrossed the Guadiana, and arrived at Torre do Mouro on the 20th of June, where the principal part of the British army was drawn up in position, with its right upon Elvas and the left on Campo Mayor. The division broke up from the bivouac at Torre do Mouro on the 21st of July, marched to Elvas, and on the following day went into quarters in Borba, from whence it marched on the 1st of September, arriving on the 3rd of that month at Portalegre.

1811

Meanwhile the main body of the army, under Viscount Wellington, had crossed the Tagus and invested *Ciudad Rodrigo*. Towards the end of September, Marshal Marmont, having received large reinforcements, advanced to Ciudad Rodrigo, and, after a partial engagement at El Bodon on the 25th of September, Viscount Wellington withdrew his army to his former position on the Coa.

On the 7th of October, a draft of one hundred and ninety-nine rank and file was received from the second battalion.

The second battalion embarked at Belfast on the 10th of October, and arrived on the following day at Irvine in North Britain.

General Girard's division of the fifth French corps having taken post at Caceres, Lieut.-General Rowland Hill determined to drive the enemy from thence, and on the approach of the British troops the French retired, halting at *Arroyo-del-Molinos*.

On the 22nd of October, the first battalion of the NINETY-SECOND marched from Portalegre to Codesiera; on the 23rd to Albuquerque; on the 24th to the Sierra de San Pedro; on the 25th to Aliseda; on the 26th to Malpartida; on the following day to Alcuesca, and bivouacked without fires about a league from *Arroyo-del-Molinos*. During the whole of this fatiguing march, the weather was extremely severe, with constant rain.

1811 The British troops, under Lieut.-General Hill, marched about two o'clock in the morning of the 28th of October, towards *Arroyo-del-Molinos*, a village situated in a plain at the foot of a ridge of rocks rising in the form of a crescent, their approach being concealed by a thick mist with heavy rain. The French infantry were assembling outside the village to commence there march to Merida, the baggage was being loaded, and General Girard was waiting at his quarters for his horse, when suddenly the *seventy-first* and NINETY-SECOND regiments charged into the village, capturing much baggage and many prisoners; at the same time the *twenty-eighth* and *thirty-fourth* regiments made a detour, supported by the *thirty-ninth*, to cut off the enemy's retreat.

The French formed two squares and commenced retreating. The NINETY-SECOND attacked, and broke one of the enemy's squares, which was formed on the other side of the village, and thereby completed his overthrow.

In this brilliant affair the enemy lost all his artillery and baggage; and several officers of rank and consideration, with about fourteen hundred men, were taken prisoners. General Brun and Colonel the Prince d'Aremberg were among the prisoners. The ninth and thirteenth light dragoons, and the second Hussars, King's German Legion, also shared in the action.

The NINETY-SECOND had Lieut.-Colonel John Cameron, Captains Donald McDonald, John McPherson, and Robert Nugent Dunbar (Brevet Major), wounded; three rank and file were killed and seven wounded.

In the evening the battalion marched to San Pedro, and on the 29th of October proceeded to Merida; on the 31st to Montejo; on the 1st of November to

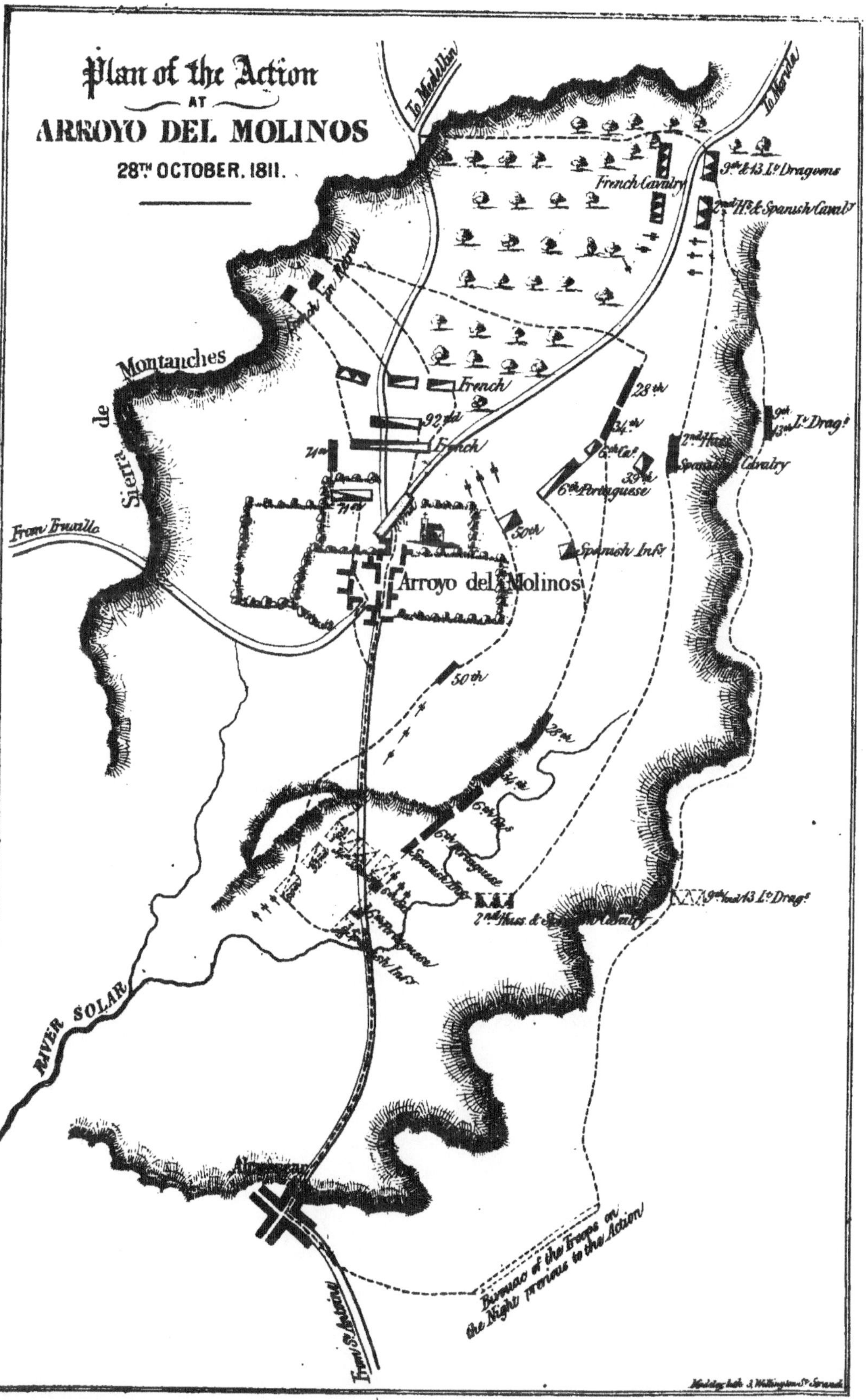
Plan of the Action
at
ARROYO DEL MOLINOS
28th OCTOBER. 1811.
To Medellin
To Merida
French Cavalry
9th & 13 Lt Dragoons
2nd H. & Spanish Cavalry
Montanches
Sierra de
French
92nd
French
71st
28th
34th
6th Cas
39th
6th Portuguese
2nd Huss
Spanish Cavalry
9th 13th Lt Drags
From Truxillo
50th
Spanish Infy
Arroyo del Molinos
50th
28th
34th
6th Portuguese
Spanish Infy
2nd Huss. & Spanish Cavalry
9th and 13 Lt Drags
RIVER SOLAR
Bivouac of the Troops on the Night previous to the Action

Campo Mayor; on the 3rd to Arronches; and arrived at Portalegre on the 4th of November.

Lieut.-General Hill, on the 7th of November, issued the following General Order:—

"Portalegre, 7th November, 1811.

" Lieut.-General Hill has great satisfaction in con-
" gratulating the troops on the success which has
" attended their recent operations in Estremadura, and
" in so doing, he cannot but endeavour to do justice to
" the merits of those through whose exertions it has
" been obtained. A patient willing endurance of forced
" and night marches, during the worst of weather and
" over bad roads, of bivouacs in wet weather, often-
" times without cover and without fire, and a strict
" observance of discipline, are qualities, however com-
" mon in British soldiers, which the Lieut.-General
" cannot pass unnoticed. Having on this occasion
" witnessed the exertion of them in no ordinary de-
" gree, he feels that nothing but the most zealous
" attention of commanding officers, the good-will and
" zealous spirit of the non-commissioned officers and
" soldiers, could produce such an effect, and he re-
" quests they will, generally and individually, accept
" his warmest thanks, particularly those corps which
" were engaged in the action of *Arroyo-del-Molinos*,
" whose silent attention to orders, when preparing to
" attack, and when manœuvring before the enemy,
" could not but excite his notice, and give them an
" additional claim on him."

Letters from the Secretary of State, dated the 2nd, and from His Royal Highness the Commander-in-Chief, dated the 6th December, were promulgated, expressive of His Royal Highness the Prince Regent's approbation and thanks to Lieut.-General Hill, and

1811 the troops under his command, for their brilliant operations on the recent expedition in Spanish Estremadura, in having totally surprised and defeated the enemy under General Girard.

Viscount Wellington having made preparations for the recapture of *Ciudad Rodrigo*, concentrated the main body of the army in that neighbourhood, and the troops under Lieut.-General Hill were therefore ordered to divert the enemy's attention in the south.

Lieut.-General Hill marched from Portalegre on the 26th of December, and proceeded on the 29th to a bivouac about a league beyond La Nava, at which village about three hundred French infantry were discovered running to their arms upon the approach of the head of the British cavalry column. They, however, effected their escape to Merida, from which place they had been that morning detached, and acquainted General Dombrouski of the approach of the British troops.

On the 30th of December, the NINETY-SECOND and other British troops entered Merida, the French having retreated during the night, where they halted during the following day.

1812 On the 1st of January, 1812, the British troops moved upon Almendralejos, beyond which, and close to the town, the enemy's columns were formed, and seen immediately retreating to Azauchal. On the 3rd, Lieut.-General Hill marched his force to Villa Franca. A brigade of infantry, and the cavalry, were pushed forward to Fuentes del Maestre, where a smart affair took place, the enemy retreating upon Llerena with the loss of some prisoners.

Lieut.-General Hill's division returned to Almendralejos on the 4th of January, and the NINETY-SECOND marched on the following day to Merida, where the troops went into quarters. The siege of *Ciudad Rodrigo*, which commenced on the 8th of January, being in a state of forwardness, it was expected that the French would make an effort to relieve the place. Lieut.-General Hill was therefore directed to throw a part of his force across the Tagus.

1812

The troops accordingly marched on the 13th of January from Merida to La Nava; on the 14th to Zogalla; on the 15th to Albuquerque; on the 16th to Codesiera; on the 17th to Portalegre; on the 19th to Alpalhão; on the 20th to Niza; and on the following day they crossed the Tagus at Villa Velha; marched from thence to Sarnadas, and on the 22nd to Castello Branco. During this march intelligence was received of the storm and capture of *Ciudad Rodrigo* by the British on the 19th of January.

On the 2nd of February, the NINETY-SECOND and other regiments under Lieut. General Hill, were directed to return to Portalegre, where they arrived on the 5th of that month.

The strength of the first battalion at this period consisted of forty-three serjeants, sixteen drummers, and seven hundred and thirty rank and file. On the 4th of March the battalion marched to Alegrete, and on the following day to Albuquerque.

Previously to this time, a large quantity of artillery stores and the battering train had been embarked at Lisbon for the Mediterranean (as it was then reported), but the vessels put into the Bay of Setuval; the whole being landed at Alcacer de Sal, and conveyed up the Alemtejo, soon appeared moving on the plains in front and to the right of Elyas, in one long and continued chain towards the Guadiana. The army now became

1812 aware that the third siege of *Badajoz* was to be undertaken.

Lieut.-General Hill's corps marched from Albuquerque on the 15th of March, and arrived at La Nava on the 16th;—proceeded on the following day to Merida, where some officers and men of the enemy were made prisoners. The division continued its march to Almendralejos on the 18th of March, where the NINETY-SECOND and other troops were stationed to cover the siege of Badajoz, before which ground had been broken on the previous day.

The division proceeded on the 21st of March from Almendralejos to Merida, and on the 26th advanced towards Medellin and Don Benito, from which places it forced the enemy to retire. Advices were here received, that the enemy, under Marshal Soult, was advancing to Llerena, with a view to relieve Badajoz, to the vicinity of which place the covering army was directed to retire.

On the 31st of March, the division proceeded towards Merida, where it arrived on the 2nd of April; it marched on the 5th to a position near Talavera Real. On the night of the 6th of April, Badajoz was assaulted and carried by the troops under the Earl of Wellington, Marshal Soult consequently retraced his steps towards Seville.

The battalion marched into quarters in Almendralejos on the 13th of April. A French force having made an irruption into the province of Beira, the Earl of Wellington, with the main body of the army, crossed the Tagus immediately after the fall of Badajoz.

On the 12th of May, the battalion marched from Almendralejos, and bivouacked near Merida; on the 13th near Arroyo-del-Molinos; on the 14th near Villa

Mesias; on the 15th entered Truxillo, and marched again about midnight; on the 16th bivouacked near Jaraicejo, and on the following day proceeded to the mountains near Casas del Puerto.

On the 18th of May, the NINETY-SECOND marched at night to attack the enemy's fortifications covering the bridge of *Almaraz*. The ruggedness of the footpath through the mountains, and the darkness of the night, presented serious obstacles to a rapid march; it was consequently daylight before the troops were formed in the Valle de Canas.

The fiftieth regiment and a wing of the seventy-first were formed in one column, and were destined to assault Fort Napoleon on the 19th of May; while the NINETY-SECOND under Lieut.-Colonel Cameron, and the other wing of the seventy-first, were formed in a second column, ready to support the attack on Fort Napoleon, or to carry the *tête-de-pont* at the same moment, both columns being provided with scaling ladders.

Fort Napoleon was carried in gallant style by the column sent against it, the enemy flying from it towards the *tête-de-pont*; the NINETY-SECOND dashed forward and entered with him. The commandant of Fort Ragusa, on the opposite bank of the Tagus, being seized with a panic, had cut away the bridge of boats; many of his countrymen consequently were either drowned or made prisoners.

The attention of all was now directed to the passage of the river. Some of the NINETY-SECOND immediately leaped in, and swam to the opposite side, bringing the boats back with them.* Thus was the bridge secured,

---

* At Almaraz on the 19th of May, 1812, the individual merit and gallantry of Privates James Gall and John Somerville of the Grena-

1812 together with Fort Ragusa, which the enemy immediately abandoned.

The enemy attached great importance to his establishment at this place, which secured the only direct communication between his two armies, and its destruction had the effect of placing them several days' march more distant from each other, and over mountainous roads hardly passable by artillery. The works and bridge at *Almaraz* having been destroyed, and about five hundred prisoners secured, the troops returned to Jaraicejo.

To commemorate the gallantry of the NINETY-SECOND in the above enterprise, the Royal Authority was afterwards received for the word "ALMARAZ" to be borne on the Regimental Colour and Appointments.

On the 21st of May, the troops marched to Truxillo, where they halted for two days. At this period intelligence was received that the French had pressed forward towards Almendralejos.

On the 24th of May, the corps under Lieut.-General Sir Rowland Hill marched to a bivouac near Villa Mesias; on the 25th proceeded to the vicinity of Rio del Agua; on the 26th to near San Pedro, and occupied quarters in Merida on the day following.

The NINETY-SECOND marched from Merida on the 5th of June, and went into quarters in Almendralejos. On the 12th of June it marched to Fuentes del Maestre, and on the following day proceeded to Puebla de Sancho Perez. The enemy having moved from

---

dier Company of the NINETY-SECOND regiment, were brought under the notice of the Commander-in-Chief as having tended to forward, in a very considerable degree, the object of Lord Hill upon Fort Ragusa: his Lordship ordered two doubloons to be given to these soldiers on the field, being the first men who leaped into the river.

Andalusia in some force, evinced an inclination to bring 1812 on an action in this advanced position, probably to divert the Earl of Wellington from his operations upon Salamanca, with which place Marshal Soult had no direct communication since the loss of the bridge of Almaraz, and every movement in advance threw him farther from co-operating with Marshal Marmont.

The battalion retired to Los Santos on the 16th of June; on the 17th to Santa Martha; and on the 18th to a wood in front of Albuhera, where all the infantry under Lieut.-General Sir Rowland Hill were assembled; some field-works were immediately thrown up to strengthen the position, and enable the Earl of Wellington, without apprehension for the safety of that corps, to prosecute his attack upon the enemy's forts at *Salamanca*, which were captured on the 27th of June.

On the 2nd of July, the battalion advanced to Santa Martha; on the 3rd it marched to a bivouac near Villa Alva, where the enemy brought up some guns, and cannonaded the troops; on the 4th it bivouacked near Feria; on the 5th near Bienvenida; on the 6th near Villa Garcia; and on the 7th it entered Llerena.

The NINETY-SECOND marched from Llerena, by Ahones, on the 8th of July to Berlenga, where some cannonading and a cavalry skirmish took place, after which the enemy retired, and the battalion returned on the following day to Llerena.

The battalion again marched from Llerena on the 20th of July to Bienvenida, and on the following day to Zafra. The enemy at this time moved to his right, and had a force near Fuentes del Maestre.

During the night of the 28th of July, the NINETY-SECOND marched towards Villa Franca, near which place the battalion bivouacked about daylight. The

1812 French were about a league in front at Fuentes del Maestre. Between nine and ten o'clock in the morning of the 29th of July, a brigade of French guns was drawn up on a height, in front of their position, and fired a royal salute. Many were the surmises as to the cause of this rejoicing, until some of the British officers ascertained at the outposts, that the salute was in honor of a victory supposed to have been gained by the French at *Salamanca*.

Lieut.-General Sir Rowland Hill, however, received more authentic intelligence from the scene of action, and immediately afterwards issued the following order:—

"*Villa Franca*, 29*th July*, 1812.

" Captain Maxwell's brigade of artillery will fire a
" salute of twenty-one guns at twelve o'clock, being in
" honor of the glorious and important victory gained
" over the enemy at *Salamanca*, by the army under the
" immediate command of the Earl of Wellington, on
" the 22nd instant.

" An extra ration of wine or spirits is to be issued
" to the British and Portuguese troops, to enable them
" to drink the Earl of Wellington's health.

(Signed) " J. C. ROOK,
" *Assistant Adjutant-General.*"

The troops were under arms, and after the salute, Lieut.-General Sir Rowland Hill advanced; the enemy, however, did not await this proof that the victory was on the side of the Allies, but immediately retired, and Fuentes del Maestre was occupied by the British troops.

On the 1st of August, the battalion went into quarters in Villa Franca.

The allied army under the Marquis of Wellington, 1812 which title was conferred upon him after the victory of Salamanca, entered Madrid on the 12th of August, and was received with every demonstration of joy by the inhabitants. Marshal Soult, in consequence of this movement, raised the blockade of Cadiz, and abandoning Western Andalusia, moved towards Grenada.

Lieut.-General Sir Rowland Hill's corps, of which the NINETY-SECOND formed part, advanced on the 28th of August to Usagre; on the 29th to Villa Garcia; on the 30th proceeded to the left to Maquilla; on the 31st to El Campillo; on the 1st of September the troops marched to Zalamea; on the 2nd to Quintana; on the 3rd to La Nava; and on the 4th to quarters in Don Benito.

On the 13th of September, Lieut.-General Sir Rowland Hill crossed the Guadiana, and marched to Mojadas; on the 14th to Villa Mesias; and on the 15th to Truxillo, where the troops halted.

The troops resumed their march from Truxillo to a bivouac near Jaraicejo on the 19th of September, and on the day following crossed a pontoon bridge thrown over the Tagus, where that of the enemy formerly stood, and bivouacked near Almaraz; on the 21st the division proceeded to Naval Moral; on the 22nd marched to Calzada de Oropeza; on the 23rd to La Gartera, and there halted.

On the 26th of September, Lieut.-General Sir Rowland Hill's division marched to Talavera de la Reinha; on the 27th to Cebolla; on the 28th to Torrijos; on the 29th to Toledo; on the 30th to a bivouac near Villa Mejor; and on the 1st of October to quarters in Aranjuez.

At this period, the Marquis of Wellington was

1812 engaged in the siege of the Castle of Burgos. Information was also received that Marshal Soult and King Joseph, with their united armies, were advancing from Valencia, and that their advanced guard was in the neighbourhood of Ocanna, and moving on Madrid.

In consequence of the necessity of raising the siege of the Castle of Burgos, and retreating, the NINETY-SECOND, and other corps under Lieut.-General Sir Rowland Hill, moved from Aranjuez on the 23rd of October, crossed the Tagus, and marched to Colominarde Orejo; on the 25th advanced to the bridge of Fuentes Duenna; on the 27th of October, the enemy appeared on the opposite bank of the river and reconnoitred. The troops under Lieut.-General Sir Rowland Hill marched on the following day to Villa Conejos, and on the same evening crossed the Jarama at Puente Larga, and went into position; on the 29th they marched to a bivouac near Valle de Moro; on the 30th near Abavaca; and on the 31st to El Escurial. The Marquis of Wellington, with the main body of the army, was at this period returning from the neighbourhood of Burgos towards Salamanca.

The NINETY-SECOND marched to a bivouac near the village of Guadarama on the 1st of November; on the 2nd crossed the Guadarama mountains, and bivouacked at Villa Castine; on the 3rd at Blasco Sancho; on the 4th at Naveos Duenna; on the 5th at Canaracillo; on the 7th crossed the river at *Alba de Tormes*, and bivouacked. On the 8th of November, the battalion was ordered into the town of Alba de Tormes to defend it, the allied army being at this time concentrated between that place and Salamanca.

The French, under Joseph Buonaparte, appeared on the 10th of November in great force on the heights above, and close to *Alba de Tormes;* after reconnoitring the place, the enemy commenced a very hot cannonade from a numerous artillery; at the same time pushing forward his light troops close under the old walls of the town, his columns ready to advance at the first appearance of the British being staggered by the effects of his artillery and numerous sharpshooters.

No such opportunity occurred, and the enemy withdrew his guns, after firing upwards of fifteen hundred shot and shell in about three hours. Such was the steadiness of the brigade, that he could not venture on the assault of a place surrounded by an old Moorish wall, in a state of perfect ruin, assailable at all points, and without any other defence than the brave troops that lined it. A strong force was kept watching the motions of the allies, and the enemy's light troops kept up a skirmish during the 11th, 12th, and 13th of November.

The NINETY-SECOND had eight rank and file killed; Lieutenant Andrew Will and thirty-three rank and file were wounded.

At daylight on the morning of the 14th of November, the enemy's cavalry were seen crossing the Tormes, about a league above the town, which was evacuated in the course of the day; the bridge blown up, and a small Spanish garrison left in the castle. This night the NINETY-SECOND bivouacked on the Arapiles, the whole army being there in position.

On the 15th of November, the enemy appeared in force about Mozarbes, and his numerous cavalry was observed moving to its left, upon the British line of communication with Ciudad Rodrigo. Towards evening the allied troops were directed to retire from the right, and the NINETY-SECOND bivouacked in a wood behind

1812 the Rio Valmuza; on the 16th near Matilla; and on the 17th behind the Rio Cuebra. During these days, the rear guard was engaged in affairs with the enemy's cavalry and light artillery. On the 18th the battalion bivouacked near Moraesverde; on the 19th marched to Zamarra; on the 20th to Robledo, and halted.

The weather had been very severe during the last few days, and the troops suffered much from its effects, being obliged several times in each day to wade through rivers, which had no existence at other seasons of the year.

The NINETY-SECOND marched to San Payo on the 28th of November; on the following day to Perales; and on the 30th to Casas de Don Gomez. On the 1st of December it went into winter quarters in Coria, where a detachment of two serjeants and thirty-six rank and file joined from the second battalion, which was at this period stationed in Scotland.

The strength of the first battalion of the NINETY-SECOND regiment now consisted of thirty-seven serjeants, fourteen drummers, and six hundred and forty-five rank and file.

1813   On the 17th of January, 1813, the battalion marched from Coria to Montehermosa, and on the 13th of February it marched to Guejo, thence to Aldea Nueva, and on the 15th to Puerta de Bannos. This movement took place in consequence of the advance of a French force from Salamanca towards Bejar, into which place some troops were thrown, and the enemy, then close to the town, retired. He, however, returned with an increased force shortly afterwards, and in the night attempted to surprise the garrison of Bejar, consisting of the *fiftieth regiment*, and the *sixth Portugese Caçadores*, by which he was repulsed with loss. The first battalion of the NINETY-SECOND regiment was put in motion to their support, and the same evening returned to its quarters in Bannos.

1813

While stationed at Bannos in April, the NINETY-SECOND received a draft of forty-six men from the second battalion. The effective strength at this period consisted of forty-four serjeants, fifteen drummers, and eight hundred and seventeen rank and file.

On the 20th of May, the NINETY-SECOND marched from Bannos to Bejar; on the 21st to Valle de Fuentes; on the 24th to Fuenteroble; on the 25th to Calzadilla; and on the following day crossed the Tormes, above Salamanca, from which place the enemy retired with the loss of some men and artillery. On the 27th of May, the NINETY-SECOND, and other corps under Lieut.-General Sir Rowland Hill, passed the Marquis of Wellington in review order, and marched to Orvado, where they halted.

The NINETY-SECOND marched on the 3rd of June from the camp at Orvado, crossed the Guarena, and encamped near Villa Buena; on the 4th the battalion crossed the Douro at Toro, and marched to Morales; on the 5th to Villa Sexmil; on the 6th to Mucientes, leaving Valladolid to the right; on the 7th to Duenas; on the 8th to Torre Quemada; on the 9th to Quintana del Ponte; on the 10th crossed the Pisuerga, and marched to Pedroza; on the 11th to Valbases; on the 12th to Celada del Camino; and on the 13th to Villa Ricos, on which morning, about daylight, the enemy blew up the Castle of Burgos, and retreated.

On the 14th of June, the battalion marched to Villa Toro; on the 15th to Villa Esquiar; on the 16th it crossed the Ebro, and marched to Pesquez; on the 17th it marched to Villa Mor; on the 18th to

1813 Boveano; on the 19th to Alcoide; and on the 20th to Robeo.

In the meantime, the French army, commanded by King Joseph, had taken up a position in the neighbourhood of *Vittoria*, where the Marquis of Wellington determined to attack the enemy.

Accordingly, on the 21st of June, the first battalion of the NINETY-SECOND regiment, under the command of Lieut.-Colonel Cameron, quitted its encampment early in the morning, and moved to La Puebla, where it crossed the river Zadorra, and ascended the mountain behind the village, which the Spaniards named "*Alturas de los Inglezes*," from an action fought there by the English in 1367, when Edward the Black Prince proceeded to Spain to assist Peter, King of Castile, to recover his throne.*

The memorable battle of *Vittoria* commenced by Lieut.-General Sir Rowland Hill obtaining possession of the heights of *La Puebla*, on which the enemy's left rested. The enemy immediately sent a reinforcement of about seven thousand men, with some artillery to this point, and made several attempts to recover his lost ground, but was as frequently repulsed by the troops which were opposed to him; and by that means they covered the remainder of the second division, while filing across the Zadorra, and in its movement to

---

* " The hill thus carried was called the Englishmen's Hill, not, as
" some recent writers have supposed, in commemoration of a victory
" gained by the Black Prince, but because of a disaster which there
" befel a part of his army. His battle was fought between Navarrette
" and Najera, many leagues from Vittoria, and beyond the Ebro;
" but on this hill the two gallant knights, Sir Thomas and Sir William
" Felton, took post with two hundred companions, and being surrounded by Don Tello with six thousand, all died or were taken
" after a long, desperate, and heroic resistance."—(History of the Peninsular War, by Major-General Sir William Napier, K.C.B.)

attack the enemy in the village of *Subijana de Alava*. 1813 Each corps kept its ground with coolness and steadiness, until everything was prepared on the left, and the allied army advanced across the plain.

At this juncture, the NINETY-SECOND was again directed to advance, and drive the enemy from every post in its front, which duty it performed in its usual manner, and the French having given way at all points, the battalion continued a rapid pursuit along the Pampeluna road, until about midnight, when it was halted near Ganuz.

On this occasion, the French suffered a great loss of men, together with all their artillery, baggage, and stores. King Joseph, whose carriage and court-equipage being seized, had barely time to escape on horseback. The defeat was the most complete that the French had experienced in Spain.

The bâton of Marshal Jourdan was taken by the eighty-seventh regiment, and the Prince Regent, in the name and behalf of His Majesty, appointed the Marquis of Wellington a Field Marshal. In a most flattering letter, the Prince thus conferred the honor: " You have sent me among the trophies of your un- " rivalled fame, the staff of a French Marshal, and I " send you in return that of England."

In commemoration of the share the NINETY-SECOND bore in gaining this signal victory, the royal authority was afterwards received for the word " VITTORIA," to be inscribed on the regimental colour and appointments. A medal was also conferred on the commanding officer, Lieut.-Colonel John Cameron.

The NINETY-SECOND had four rank and file killed, and sixteen wounded.

On the 22nd of June, the allies followed the re-

1813 treating enemy, on which day the NINETY-SECOND marched to about a league in front of Salvatierra, and encamped; on the 23rd proceeded to near Arbeniz; on the 24th to near Araquil; on the 25th to near Stormende; on the 26th to near Zuaza; and on the 27th marched to Orcayen, about three miles from *Pampeluna*, which latter place was afterwards invested.

The NINETY-SECOND marched to a wood near Lizasso on the 2nd of July; on the 3rd to Puerta Velate; on the 4th to *Almandoz*, where a skirmish took place, the enemy being in position between Beruete and Aniz. On the 5th, after some movements to turn the left of his position, he retreated, and the NINETY-SECOND bivouacked in front of Elizondo, halting there during the following day.

On the 7th of July, the enemy was seen in a strong position on the heights of *Maya*, and troops were sent across the Bidassoa to attack his right. The NINETY-SECOND marched through the village of Maya in the afternoon, and a good deal of fighting took place during the day, the light troops continuing to skirmish until dark, when the battalion bivouacked.

Advancing early in the morning of the 8th of July, the French retired from their *own* frontier, which the pursuing troops occupied with three British cheers. The light troops continued the pursuit towards the village of Urdax.

On the 9th of July, the troops marched to the village of Maya. The siege of *St. Sebastian* was undertaken, and the garrison of *Pampeluna* was closely invested by the Spaniards at this period.

Upon Napoleon receiving the news of the defeat of the French at Vittoria, he immediately sent Marshal Soult to Spain, with the rank of " Lieutenant of the

Emperor," and the Marshal assumed the command of the army of Spain on the 12th of July. All his energies were directed to retrieve its disasters, and to drive the British across the Ebro.

1818

On the 13th of July, the first brigade, at this period under the command of Lieut.-Colonel Cameron, of the NINETY-SECOND, marched to occupy the heights of *Maya.*

The effective strength of the battalion, under the command of Major James Mitchell, consisted of forty serjeants, fifteen drummers, and seven hundred and sixty-two rank and file, on the 25th of July, on which day the fiftieth regiment was stationed on the right of the brigade, to the left of a pass leading to the village of Maya, which was occupied by a piquet from the second brigade.

The NINETY-SECOND were stationed in the Maya Pass, to the right of the road leading from Urdax, and the seventy-first regiment still further to the left. The enemy collected a force of about fifteen thousand men behind some rocky ground in front of the British right, and with this overwhelming force drove in the light companies of the second brigade, gaining the high rock on the right of the allied position before the arrival of the second brigade from Maya, which was, therefore, compelled to retrace its steps towards the village, instead of falling back to its left on the first brigade.

Lieut.-Colonel Cameron, detached the fiftieth to the right the moment the action commenced. That regiment was severely engaged, and was forced to retire along the ridge; the right wing of the NINETY-SECOND, under Major John McPherson, was sent to its support, and for some time had to stand the whole brunt of the

1813 enemy's column. The right wing of the seventy-first regiment was also brought up, but such was the advantage of the position the enemy had gained by separating the two brigades, and in a manner descending upon the Pass of Maya, while a fresh division was pushing up to it from the direction of Urdax, that the small body of troops received orders to retire to a high rock on the left of the position.

This movement was covered by the left wings of the seventy-first and NINETY-SECOND regiments, which, relieving each other with the utmost order and regularity, and disputing every inch of ground, left nothing for the enemy to boast of. The brigade continued to hold the rock until the arrival of Major-General Edward Barnes's brigade, when a general charge was made, and every inch of ground recovered as far as the Maya Pass.

On this occasion the NINETY-SECOND was ordered by Lieut.-General the Honorable Sir William Stewart not to charge, the battalion having been hotly engaged for ten successive hours, and in want of ammunition. The NINETY-SECOND, however, for the first time disregarded an order, and not only charged, but led the charge.

During the whole of the action on the 25th of July, the conduct of the NINETY-SECOND was most noble and devoted; and in commemoration of which His Majesty was pleased to permit Lieut.-Colonel Cameron to bear on his shield the word "MAYA." Lieut.-Colonel John Cameron and Major James Mitchell were both wounded at the head of the battalion, and the command devolved on Major John McPherson, who was also wounded, but did not leave the field. The other officers wounded were Captains George W. Holmes, Ronald McDonald, and Samuel Bevan,

Lieutenants William Fyfe, Donald McPherson, John A. Durie, James John Chisholm, Robert Winchester, Donald McDonald, James Ker Ross, George Gordon, John Grant, and Alexander McDonald, (died) and Ensigns Thomas Mitchell and George Mitchell.

1813

Ensign Ewen Kennedy was killed. The other casualties were thirty-four rank and file killed, and two hundred and sixty eight rank and file wounded; and twenty-two rank and file missing.

Major-General Sir William Napier, in his History of the Peninsular War, in narrating the action in the Pass of Maya, has alluded to the loss of the battalion, and its gallantry, in the following terms :—

" And that officer (Lieut.-Colonel Cameron) still " holding the Pass of Maya with the left wings of the " seventy-first and NINETY-SECOND regiments, brought " their right wings and the Portuguese guns into action, " and thus maintained the fight; but so dreadful was " the slaughter, especially of the NINETY-SECOND, that " it is said the advancing enemy was actually stopped " by the heaped mass of dead and dying." * * *

" The stern valour of the NINETY-SECOND would have " graced Thermopylæ." * * * * *

The enemy having turned the British position at Roncesvalles, the troops were withdrawn. The first battalion of the NINETY-SECOND was ordered to march from Puerto de Maya, and arrived in position at Iruite early in the morning of the 26th of July.

The troops composing the right of the allied army at Roncesvalles, having retired towards Pampeluna, the NINETY-SECOND marched, on the 27th of July, from its position near Iruite, and halted between Puerta Velate and Lanz. On the following day, the battalion marched to a bivouac near Lizasso, and, on the 29th, marched somewhat further towards Pampeluna.

1813 On the 30th of July, the battalion advanced to a position between the village of *Lizasso* and *Eguaros*, when the enemy appeared at the former place, and commenced an extended movement upon the British left. The NINETY-SECOND, under the command of Major John McPherson, was directed against him, and found itself opposed to a column of about two thousand men, which the battalion immediately charged, and drove from the ridge in a most gallant style. After this the French moved still further to their right, and accordingly the left of the allies was thrown back in the direction of Arestegui. The action ceased about dark.

The NINETY-SECOND had Captain George W. Holmes wounded. Nine rank and file were killed, and twenty-six wounded.

The NINETY-SECOND advanced, and on the 31st of July, came up with the enemy strongly posted on a hill at *Dona Maria*, which could only be approached by a narrow ziz-zag road through very close underwood. In this favorable position the enemy made great resistance, but was ultimately driven from the heights, and his defeat was particularly ascribed to the persevering bravery individually displayed in the ranks of the NINETY-SECOND regiment.

Lieut-General Sir Rowland Hill, under whose eye the battalion was this day engaged, bestowed the most flattering encomiums on its gallantry. On this occasion Major McPherson was wounded, and Captain James Seaton assumed the command. Captains James Lee and Dugald Campbell, Lieutenant James Hope, and Ensign Thomas Mitchell, were also wounded. Ten rank and file were killed, and sixty-nine wounded.

After carrying this post, the NINETY-SECOND moved towards Lanz, and, on the 1st of August, marched through the pass at Lanz to Ariscun, and on the 2nd, 1813 again occupied the heights of Maya.

The royal authority was subsequently granted for the NINETY-SECOND to bear the word "PYRENEES" on the regimental colour and appointments, to commemorate the services of the first battalion in these combats, which have been designated the "*Battles of the Pyrenees.*" Medals, bearing the word "PYRENEES," were conferred on Major John McPherson and Captain James Seaton; and the former was promoted to the brevet rank of Lieut.-Colonel.

The effective strength of the NINETY-SECOND was now reduced to twenty-seven serjeants, fifteen drummers, and three hundred and twenty rank and file. The battalion marched on the evening of the 2nd of August to the village of Erassu, and on the 5th re-occupied the heights of Maya.

On the 8th of August, the NINETY-SECOND marched from Maya to the valley of Alduides, and the next day to Roncesvalles, between which place and the heights of Don Carlos, the battalion remained encamped until the beginning of November.

In the meantime, *St. Sebastian* and *Pampeluna* had been captured, and the British commander, looking down from the lofty Pyrenees on the well-guarded territory of France, resolved to carry the war into the heart of that country.

On the 7th of November, the enemy made an attempt to cut off a piquet of the NINETY-SECOND, but was foiled. On the following day, the battalion marched from Roncesvalles to Alduides, and on the 9th proceeded through Maya to Urdax, in which neighbourhood the whole division was assembled.

The British army was put in motion at an early

1813 hour in the morning of the 10th of November, and advanced to attack the enemy in his fortified position on the *Nivelle*. The NINETY-SECOND, under the command of Lieut.-Colonel Cameron, forded that river a little below Ainhoe, and was ordered to attack the strong redoubts on the heights immediately in rear of the village.

The action became very warm towards the centre of the British line, and the sixth division, with the Portuguese division immediately on the left, having turned the redoubts to the right of the enemy's position on the heights of Ainhoe, the French in front of the NINETY-SECOND made little resistance, running out of the redoubts in the utmost confusion; the enemy giving way at all points, left the allies a complete victory, and abandoned all his artillery and stores. The NINETY-SECOND occupied the huts in the French position for the night, and the next day advanced to Espelette.

On the 12th of November, the division moved in advance to reconnoitre the enemy at Cambo, and after driving in his outposts and effecting the object in view, the NINETY-SECOND bivouacked at a short distance from the town.

The battalion went into quarters in Cambo on the 16th of November; the enemy having previously blown up the bridge, retired across the *Nive*, leaving some pieces of heavy artillery behind.

On the 27th of November, a detachment of one hundred men joined from the second battalion, which still remained in Scotland.

The rivers, which had been greatly swollen by the rains, having partly subsided, the allied army was put in motion across the *Nive* on the 9th of December.

The NINETY-SECOND, commanded by Lieut.-Colonel 1813 Cameron, forded that river near Cambo, but did not meet with much opposition, as the enemy retired to prevent his retreat to Bayonne from being cut off by the sixth division, which was crossing lower down the river. The NINETY-SECOND advanced on the same day to Urcuray: on the 10th and 11th, the French attacked the troops on the left of the Nive, but on each day were repulsed.

On the 11th of December, the NINETY-SECOND advanced to Petite Moguerre, a small village near Bayonne, situated between the rivers Nive and Adour.

The enemy was observed at daylight in the morning of the 13th of December, formed in very heavy columns between his entrenched camp at Bayonne, and the village of St. Pierre, on the road leading to St. Jean-Pied-de-Port.

The NINETY-SECOND, under the command of Lieut.-Colonel Cameron, was ordered to advance to the centre of the position at *St. Pierre*, against which the enemy appeared to direct his principal attack. The battalion had scarcely arrived on its ground, when it was led into action, and by a most opportune and determined charge, drove the French from the British position (of which they had for a moment possessed themselves) to the very point from whence they had started.

The NINETY-SECOND was recalled to its proper position, and no sooner was it formed there, than the enemy again attacked, and was again repulsed. Besides being exposed during this day to a continued fire of musketry and artillery, the battalion made *four* distinct charges with the bayonet, each time driving the enemy to his original position in front of his entrenchments.

Lieut. General the Honorable Sir William Stewart,

1813 K.B., in his report of the action, stated, that "several "brilliant charges were made by our troops in the "centre, against which the enemy's principal attack "was directed, more particularly that by the NINETY-"SECOND Highlanders."

In speaking of the defeat of the enemy's principal attack on the road to St. Jean Pied-de-Port, where the first brigade was stationed, the Marquis of Wellington said in his despatch, "they were particularly engaged "in the contest with the enemy at that point, and these "troops conducted themselves admirably."

On this occasion Lieutenants Duncan McPherson, Thomas Mitchell, and Alan McDonald were killed. Major John McPherson (mortally), Captains George W. Holmes, Ronald McDonald, and Donald McPherson; Lieutenants John Catenaugh, Ronald McDonald, James John Chisholm, Robert Winchester, and George Mitchell, and Ensign William Fraser were wounded. Twenty-eight rank and file were killed, and one hundred and forty-three wounded.

In commemoration of this action, an honorary badge was conferred by His Majesty on Lieut.-Colonel Cameron, bearing the word "NIVE," and the senior captain of the regiment (Captain James Seaton) was promoted to the brevet rank of major. The royal authority was also granted for the NINETY-SECOND to bear the word "NIVE" on the regimental colour and appointments.

The enemy retired into Bayonne a little before dark, and the NINETY-SECOND went into its former quarters in Petite Moguerre.

On the 14th of December, the following order was issued by Lieut.-General the Honorable Sir William Stewart, K.B. :—

"Head Quarters, near Petite Moguerre,
14th December, 1813.

"The second division has greatly distinguished "themselves, and its gallantry in yesterday's action is "avowed by the Commander of the forces and the "allied army."

The NINETY-SECOND marched from Petite Moguerre on the 17th of December, and on the 19th occupied cantonments in Arquite.

On the 4th of January, 1814, the battalion marched from Arquite, and encamped near Urt; on the 8th it went into cantonments in that village. On the 20th of January the battalion marched from Urt for St. Jean de Luz, where it received new clothing, and on the 26th returned to Urt.

The enemy attacked on the 27th of January a piquet of the NINETY-SECOND, stationed in an island on the Adour, but was driven back.

At this period the allied army was put in motion, and the NINETY-SECOND marched from Urt to Urcuray.

The NINETY-SECOND, under the command of Lieut.-Colonel Cameron, marched on the 14th of February to attack a considerable body of the enemy under General Harispe at *Hellette*, which was forced to retire to Meharin. On this occasion Lieutenant Richard McDonell was wounded; one private was killed, and seven rank and file wounded.

On the morning of the 15th of February, the NINETY-SECOND marched in pursuit of the enemy, who was discovered, late in the evening, strongly posted on the heights in front of *Garris*, which the division attacked and carried in gallant style. The French obstinately disputed their ground, and made several attempts to recover it after dark, but finding the British troops

1814 immovable, they retreated with considerable loss through St. Palais. On this occasion Major James Seaton was mortally wounded, and expired on the 22nd of the following month. The other casualties were three rank and file wounded.

During the night the enemy destroyed the bridge at St. Palais, and every exertion was made to repair it. On the 16th of February, the NINETY-SECOND crossed in the afternoon, and occupied a position in advance.

On the 17th of February, the enemy was discovered in the village of *Arriverete*, on the right bank of the Gave de Mauleon, endeavouring to destroy the bridge over it. A ford was discovered a little higher up, which the NINETY-SECOND crossed under cover of the British artillery, and immediately attacking the troops in the village with its usual success, drove the enemy out of it, and secured the bridge by which the troops were enabled to cross. The enemy retired across the Gave d'Oleron, and the battalion, which had ten rank and file wounded in this enterprise, was cantoned in Arriverete and the neighbouring villages.

In honor of this occasion, it was granted by royal warrant, that Lieut.-Colonel Cameron should bear for his crest a Highlander of the NINETY-SECOND regiment, up to the middle in water, grasping in his right hand a broad sword, and in his left a banner inscribed 92nd, within a wreath of laurel; and as a motto over it the word "*Arriverete.*"

The following is an extract of the Marquis of Wellington's despatch on this occasion:—

"St. Jean de Luz, 20th February, 1814.

"The enemy retired across the river at St. Palais in
"the night, destroying the bridges, which, however,

" were repaired so that the troops under Sir Rowland 1814
" Hill crossed on the 16th, and on the 17th the enemy
" were driven across the Gave de Mauleon.

" They attempted to destroy the bridge at Arri-
" verete, but they had not time to complete its de-
" struction; and a ford being discovered above the
" bridge, the NINETY-SECOND regiment under the com-
" mand of Lieut.-Colonel Cameron, supported by the
" fire of Captain Beane's troop of horse artillery,
" crossed the ford, and made a most gallant attack
" upon two battalions of French infantry posted in the
" village, from which the latter were driven with con-
" siderable loss."

The Marquis of Wellington addressed the following letter to Lieut.-General Lord Niddry (afterwards Earl of Hopetoun), colonel of the NINETY-SECOND, relative to an application to be permitted to bear the word " ARRIVERETE" on the regimental colour and appointments:—

"Cambray, 13th April, 1816.

" MY DEAR LORD,

" I have received your letter of the
" 2nd, regarding the desire of the NINETY-SECOND regi-
" ment to bear the word " *Arriverete*" on their colour,
" &c., to which I have no objection, and I will apply
" for the distinction, if after this explanation they
" should still desire it.

" Arriverete is a village on the Gave de Mauleon,
" at which there is a wooden bridge. We had passed
" the river at other points, but our communication
" across it was difficult, and the enemy was of such a
" force at Sauveterre, in the neighbourhood, that we
" could not venture to move along it, and I wished to
" get possession of the bridge before the enemy could

1814 " destroy it. The NINETY-SECOND forded the river,
" and attacked and took the village, against a very
" superior force of the enemy, in the most gallant style,
" (in the manner in which they have always performed
" every service in which they have been employed),
" but without much loss; there the affair ended; we
" were not prepared at that time to do more, and we
" held that village as a *tête-de-pont* till our means were
" in readiness for our further operations.

" There is no doubt but the troops behaved as gal-
" lantly in this affair as they could in any of greater
" importance, but the result was not of that consequence
" to the ulterior operations of the army, to have ren-
" dered it notorious to the army at large; and although
" I reported it as I ought, I know there are many
" belonging to the army, some even who were present,
" have no recollection of the name of the place which
" was the scene of the action, and some not even of
" the action itself.

" It appears to me to be beneath the reputation of
" the NINETY-SECOND to have to explain for what cause
" the name of a particular place has been inserted in
" their colours; and notwithstanding that on no oc-
" casion could they or any other troops behave better
" than they did upon that, I acknowledge that I am
" anxious they should not press the request. But
" if after this explanation they continue to wish it,
" I will take care it shall be granted.

" I have, &c.,
(Signed) " WELLINGTON.
" Lieut.-General Lord Niddry, K.B.,
&c.,   &c."

The NINETY-SECOND marched in the morning of the 24th of February, 1814, and crossed the Gave d'Oleron by a ford near Villeneuve, and on the 25th moved on 1814 the road towards *Orthes*, and encamped near Laas, where the battalion halted. The allied army was at this period crossing the Gave de Pau, near Peyrehorade, with the exception of the corps under Lieut.-General Sir Rowland Hill.

On the 27th of February, the army under the Marquis of Wellington, on the right bank of the Gave de Pau advanced to attack the French position near *Orthes*, and the action soon became general. The first brigade, to which the NINETY-SECOND under Lieut.-Colonel Cameron belonged, was directed to a ford above the town of Orthes, and had the honor of leading the second division across the Gave de Pau, under a very heavy fire of musketry and artillery, and possessing itself of the road from Orthes to the town of Pau, immediately in rear of the enemy's left flank, his retreat on that line was consequently cut off. The NINETY-SECOND was ordered to move upon the road to St. Sever, along the rear of the enemy, whose retreat, which had been conducted hitherto with some degree of order, now became a perfectly confused flight. The pursuit was at an equally rapid pace, in which the battalion was conspicuous for several miles, until it halted at Sault de Navailles.

In commemoration of this victory, which cost the enemy twelve pieces of cannon, and about seven thousand men, the NINETY-SECOND received the royal authority to bear the word "ORTHES" on the regimental colour and appointments. His Majesty was also pleased to confer honorary badges, bearing the word "*Orthes*," on Lieut.-Colonel John Cameron, who commanded the first battalion, and on Major James Mitchell, who

1814 commanded the light companies; the latter officer was promoted to the brevet rank of lieut.-colonel.

The NINETY-SECOND had only three rank and file wounded, and one killed, in the battle of Orthes.

On the 28th of February, the NINETY-SECOND marched to St. Medard, and on the 1st of March proceeded to Grenade; the main body of the allied army had at this period crossed the Adour at St. Sever.

The enemy, on the 2nd of March, was seen strongly posted on a ridge in front of the town of *Aire*, with his right resting on the Adour. The allied army advanced to the attack, and compelled him to retire; but a brigade of Portuguese troops on the British flank giving way, the French became encouraged, and in their turn advanced. The *fiftieth* and NINETY-SECOND regiments, after clearing their own front, were moved rapidly to the point where the enemy was successful, and by a most splendid charge immediately put him to flight.

These regiments now became considerably separated from each other, from having to occupy the ground destined for the Portuguese troops, and the NINETY-SECOND was again opposed to a strong column on its flank, which it immediately charged, and pursued through the town of Aire, in which the battalion was afterwards cantoned.

Captain William Fyfe, Lieutenants John A. Durie and Richard McDonell were wounded. The other casualties of the battalion were three rank and file killed, and twenty-nine wounded.

His Majesty, in honor of this occasion, granted permission for Lieut.-Colonel Cameron to bear upon his shield a view of the town, with the word "AIRE."

The following Division and General Orders were issued, alluding to the action of this day:—

"Division Orders.   Aire, March 3rd, 1814.

"Lieut.-General Sir William Stewart con-
"gratulates the division on its further advance and
"success against the enemy. To the admirable conduct
"of the fiftieth and NINETY-SECOND regiments led by
"their gallant commanders, and by Major-General
"Barnes, the good fortune of yesterday's action is de-
"cidedly attributed, which the Lieut.-General has to
"state to Lieut.-General Sir Rowland Hill, for the in-
"formation of the Commander of the Forces."

"General Orders.   Aire, March 5th, 1814.

"Lieut.-General Sir Rowland Hill congra-
"tulates Lieut.-General Sir William Stewart, Major-
"General Barnes, and Major-General Byng, on the
"brilliant part which they bore in the action of the
"2nd instant."

"The gallant and steady conduct of the fiftieth
"regiment, under Lieut.-Colonel Harrison, and of the
"NINETY-SECOND regiment, under Lieut.-Colonel
"Cameron, excited the admiration of all who were wit-
"nesses of it."

On the 10th of March, a letter and address, of which the following are copies, were received, and promulgated to the first battalion of the NINETY-SECOND regiment.

"Dear Sir,   Aire, March 10th, 1814.

"The mayor and inhabitants of this town
"having requested me to convey to you, with their
"sentiments of gratitude, the accompanying address, I
"feel infinite pleasure in so doing; as I deem the senti-

"ments expressed in it justly due towards you, and the distinguished regiment under your command.

"I have &c.,

(Signed) "WILLIAM STEWART,
"Lieut.-General.

"Lieut.-Colonel Cameron,
Commanding NINETY-SECOND Highlanders."

(Translation.)

"SIR, Aire, 9th March, 1814.

"The inhabitants of the town of Aire are not ignorant that if they were preserved from pillage and destruction at the close of the obstinate and sanguinary conflict of the 2nd of March, they are indebted for such preservation from that calamity to your honorable conduct, and the strict discipline which you have maintained amongst the troops under your command.

"Penetrated by sentiments of the liveliest gratitude towards a commander distinguished by such noble qualities, the town of Aire has charged me to be their interpreter in communicating their thanks, and to offer you the homage of their esteem.

"I have, &c.,

(Signed) "CODROY, *Mayor.*

"To Lieut-Colonel Cameron,
Commanding NINETY-SECOND Highlanders."

Information having been received that the enemy was making a movement to his left, and attempting to throw himself upon the right flank of the British, a corresponding move was made by the Marquis of Wellington, and the NINETY-SECOND marched from Aire on the 13th of March, by the road to Pau, and halted in a position near Garlin, the French being posted behind the river Gros Lees. On the 18th, the 1814 battalion marched to Conchez, the enemy retiring towards Lembege on the approach of the allies.

The NINETY-SECOND moved upon Lembege on the 19th of March, where a skirmish took place, the enemy falling back to Vic Bigorre; here he seemed determined to make a stand, but the third division, which moved by a road to the British left, drove him in excellent style from his position, and he retired across the Adour. The battalion halted for the night in front of Vic Bigorre.

On the 20th of March, the left of the army crossed the Adour, and moved upon the enemy's right near Rabastens, while the right marched upon Tarbes, the French having retired from it, as the allied columns were forming for their attack.

The NINETY-SECOND continued in pursuit of the enemy on the main road from Tarbes to Toulouse, by St. Gaudens, Mariemont, and St. Julien, and halted on the 26th of March at Muret: there had been constant rain for several days previous, which impeded operations; on the 27th, the troops under Lieut.-General Sir Rowland Hill were withdrawn to St. Roque.

On the 31st of March, 1814, the division crossed the Garonne by a pontoon bridge, and proceeded to Miremont; on the 1st of April to Cintegabelle, and crossed the Arriege. No road for artillery could be discovered from this place to Toulouse, and the NINETY-SECOND recrossed the Garonne at St. Roque, the pontoons being removed towards Grenade.

The NINETY-SECOND marched on the 5th of April to cantonments at St. Simon. At this period the river Garonne had swollen, and this circumstance made it necessary to remove the pontoons by which part of the

1814 allied army had crossed; they were however replaced, and on the evening of the 9th of April the main body of the British army was on the right of the Garonne.

On the 10th of April, the NINETY-SECOND advanced by the Muret road to the vicinity of *Toulouse*, and drove Marshal Soult's outposts into his entrenchments on that side. The services of the battalion were not again required during this day; it however witnessed the gallant conduct of its comrades on the opposite bank of the river, driving the enemy from his redoubts above the town, and gaining a complete victory.

During the 11th of April nothing particular occurred beyond a skirmish, and confining the enemy to the suburbs. The French evacuated Toulouse during the night, and the white flag was hoisted. On the 12th of April the Marquis of Wellington entered the city amidst the acclamations of the inhabitants. The NINETY-SECOND followed the enemy on the Villa Franche road, and encamped in advance of that town.

In the course of the afternoon of the 12th of April, intelligence was received of the abdication of Napoleon: had not the express been delayed on the journey by the French police, the sacrifice of many valuable lives would have been prevented.

A disbelief in the truth of this intelligence occasioned much unnecessary bloodshed at *Bayonne*, the garrison of which made a desperate sortie on the 14th of April, and Lieut.-General Sir John Hope (afterwards Earl of Hopetoun), the Colonel of the NINETY-SECOND regiment, was taken prisoner. Major-General Andrew Hay was killed, and Major-General Stopford was wounded. This was the last action of the Peninsular war.

On the 20th of April, 1814, the NINETY-SECOND

marched into Villa Franche; on the 24th to Beziege; and on the 25th occupied quarters in Toulouse. 1814

A treaty of peace was established between Great Britain and France; Louis XVIII. was restored to the throne of France, and Napoleon Buonaparte was permitted to reside at Elba, the sovereignty of that island having been conferred upon him by the allied powers.

The war being ended, the NINETY-SECOND marched from Toulouse on the 5th of June, and continued on the move until the 19th of that month, when it encamped at Blanchfort, about two leagues from Bourdeaux.

In addition to the other distinctions acquired during the war in Spain, Portugal, and the south of France the NINETY-SECOND received the royal authority to bear, the word "PENINSULA" on the Regimental Colour and Appointments.

On the 9th of July, the NINETY-SECOND marched from Blanchfort, and encamped near Pouillac. On the 17th of July, the battalion was conveyed down the Garonne in small craft, and embarked in H.M.'s ship "Norge," which sailed immediately, and on the 26th entered Cove of Cork harbour.

The NINETY-SECOND disembarked at Monkstown on the 29th of July, and marched to Fermoy barracks, where the thanks of Parliament were communicated to the officers and soldiers for "the meritorious and " eminent services which they had rendered to their " King and Country during the course of the war."

On the 6th of August, the first battalion of the NINETY-SECOND regiment, commanded by Colonel Cameron, was inspected at Fermoy by Major-General Sir William Aylett, who expressed in orders his great satisfaction at its appearance under arms, as well as of

1814 its interior economy. Its effective strength consisted of fifty serjeants, sixteen drummers, and seven hundred rank and file.

Two captains and three lieutenants were ordered on the 12th of October to proceed to Scotland to take under their charge the non-commissioned officers and men of the second battalion, about to be transferred to the first battalion.

On the 24th of October, the second battalion of the NINETY-SECOND regiment was disbanded at Edinburgh, and twelve serjeants, thirteen drummers, and one hundred and sixty-one rank and file were transferred to the first battalion, which they joined at Fermoy in January following.

1815 The NINETY-SECOND regiment marched on the 27th of January, 1815, from Fermoy to Cork barracks, where an authority was received for the establishment to be one thousand rank and file.

The NINETY-SECOND regiment was not destined to remain long on home service. The peace of Europe was again disturbed. Napoleon Bonaparte returned from Elba, landed at Cannes, in Provence, on the 1st of March, 1815, with a handful of men, and on the 20th of that month entered Paris at the head of an army which had joined him on the road. Louis XVIII. withdrew from Paris to Ghent, and Napoleon assumed his former dignity of Emperor of the French; but the allied Powers refused to acknowledge his sovereignty, and determined on his dethronement. Preparations for war commenced accordingly, and the NINETY-SECOND regiment was ordered to proceed on foreign service.

The regiment marched to the Cove of Cork on the 1st of May, and embarked in transports, which sailed on the 3rd of May. Its effective strength consisted of forty-seven serjeants, sixteen drummers, and six hundred and twenty-one rank and file. The regiment anchored near Ostend on the 9th of May, was removed in boats on the following day, and subsequently proceeded by the canal to Bruges.

1815

On the 11th of May the regiment proceeded to Ghent, where it landed, and was quartered. Louis XVIII. was residing there at this period.

The regiment marched from Ghent to Alost on the 27th of May, and on the 28th to Brussels, where it was placed in Major-General Sir Denis Pack's brigade, with the third battalion of the Royals, the forty-second Highlanders, and the second battalion of the forty-fourth regiment.

On the 3rd of June the British brigades of the fifth division, to which the NINETY-SECOND belonged, were reviewed by Field Marshal the Duke of Wellington, who expressed his entire approbation of their appearance, and his happiness at again seeing those that had served with such reputation in the Peninsula.

Napoleon left Paris on the 12th of June, and conformably to his usual plan of directing at once his whole force against some important point, he determined to attack the British and Prussian armies before the arrival of the Austrians and Russians, who were already in movement towards the frontiers. On the 15th, intelligence having been received that the French had entered the Netherlands, the NINETY-SECOND lay upon their arms during the night.

On the 16th of June, the division under Lieut.-General Sir Thomas Picton marched at daylight, and about two o'clock came within range of the enemy's artillery in front of Genappe, at some farm-houses denominated *Les Quatre Bras,* where the main road

1815 from Charleroi to Brussels is crossed by another from Nivelles to Namur, and which served as the British communication with the Prussians on the left.

The NINETY-SECOND regiment was ordered to line a ditch in the front of this latter road, to the left of the farmhouses, and the Duke of Wellington took his station with it. The enemy poured a very hot fire of artillery on this post, and his cavalry charged it, but was received by a well-directed volley from the regiment, and forced to retire with great loss of men and horses. His cannonade still continued, and his cavalry again charged, and were repulsed as before. In the meantime the French infantry had been forming under cover of their cavalry attacks, assisted by their artillery, and now advanced upon the regiment, when the Duke of Wellington said, "NINETY-SECOND, you must charge "these fellows!" These words were scarcely uttered, when every man of the regiment sprang over the ditch, and his orders were fully and literally obeyed. The enemy was not only driven from the houses and gardens about Quatre Bras, but chased for half a mile beyond it, until the regiment was recalled about nightfall, and the action ceased.

On this occasion the regiment had to lament the loss of its commanding officer, Colonel Cameron,[*] an officer who had led the NINETY-SECOND in many a sanguinary field. He fell as he had lived, with honor;

---

[*] On the 30th of September, 1815, His Royal Highness the Prince Regent, in the name and on the behalf of His Majesty, was pleased to grant the dignity of a baronet of the United Kingdom of Great Britain and Ireland, to Ewen Cameron, Esq., of Fassifern and Callart, in the county of Argyll, and of Arthurstone, in the county of Angus, to commemorate the services of his son, Colonel Cameron, of the NINETY-SECOND regiment.

and the Duke of Wellington thus expressed himself in 1815 his despatch to Earl Bathurst of the 29th of June, transmitting lists of the killed and wounded:—

"Your Lordship will see in the enclosed lists the names of some most valuable officers lost to His Majesty's service. Among them I cannot avoid to mention Colonel Cameron, of the NINETY-SECOND, and Colonel Sir Henry Ellis, of the twenty-third regiments, to whose conduct I have frequently drawn your Lordship's attention, and who at last fell distinguishing themselves at the head of the brave troops which they commanded.

"Notwithstanding the glory of the occasion, it is impossible not to lament such men, both on account of the public, and as friends."

The Duke of Wellington particularly mentioned the twenty-eighth, forty-second, seventy-ninth, and NINETY-SECOND regiments in his account of the action at Quatre Bras.

The NINETY-SECOND regiment during the action was successively commanded by Colonel Cameron, Lieut.-Colonel James Mitchell, and Major Donald Macdonald. Colonel Cameron, Captain William Little, Lieutenant James John Chisholm, Ensigns Abel Becher, and John Ross McPherson were killed. Lieut.-Colonel James Mitchell, Captains George W. Holmes, Dugald Campbell, and William Charles Grant; Lieutenants Robert Winchester, Thomas Hobbs, Thomas McIntosh, James Ker Ross, Ronald McDonald, Hector Munro Innes, George Logan, John McKinlay, George Mackie, Alexander McPherson, Ewen Ross, Ensigns John Branwell, Robert Logan, Angus McDonald, Robert Hewitt, and assistant surgeon John Stewart were wounded. Thirty-five rank and file were killed, and two hundred and forty five were wounded.

1815 The following is a copy of Major McDonald's report of the action, written on the spot, to Major-General Sir Denis Pack, K.C.B.:—

" SIR,

"Colonel Cameron and Lieut.-Colonel Mitchell " having been both severely wounded, I have the honor " to report, for your information, (not having been " under your eye during the whole of the day,) that " the NINETY-SECOND regiment repulsed repeated " attacks of cavalry, and by a rapid movement charged " a column of the enemy, and drove them to the ex- " tremity of the wood on our right.

" Our loss has been severe, as will be seen by the " return of killed and wounded.

" I have, &c.,
(Signed) " DONALD McDONALD,
" Major 92nd, Commanding.
" Major-General
Sir Denis Pack, K.C.B."

The Prussians had been attacked on the 16th of June at Ligny, and were forced to retreat to Wavre, and the Duke of Wellington made a corresponding movement to keep up his communication with them. In the course of the morning of the 17th of June, the troops were withdrawn from Quatre Bras, and the regiment was directed to form the rear-guard of the infantry, until it occupied its position in front of *Waterloo*, at a place named Mont St. Jean, where it arrived without being molested by the enemy.

At the beginning of the memorable battle of Waterloo, which commenced about ten o'clock in the morning of the 18th of June, the NINETY-SECOND regiment, under the command of Major McDonald, with the rest of Sir Denis Pack's brigade, was placed in support of some Belgian troops on the left of the main road to Brussels, and throughout the day was 1815 exposed to the fire of the enemy's artillery and sharp-shooters.

The allied troops to the right having repulsed the repeated attacks in that quarter, the enemy directed his attention in a more particular manner to this part of the British line; and after having succeeded in carrying the farm-house of *La Haye Sainte*, under a most tremendous fire of artillery, he drove the Belgians from their post, and established himself in that part of the position. The moment the Belgians were seen running past the regiment to the rear, the third battalion of the Royals, and the second battalion of the forty-fourth regiment on its right in brigade, moved to the point which had thus been abandoned, and for some time maintained their ground in a manner becoming British soldiers, although ultimately obliged to give way. The NINETY-SECOND at this time was reduced to less than three hundred men. A column of three thousand French was formed in the position in front of the regiment, which was concealed by the nature of the ground. The French Commander having possessed himself of so advantageous a post, and seeing the troops give way, considered everything gained, and ordered arms.

This was the state of affairs, when Major-General Sir Denis Pack galloped up to the regiment, and called out "NINETY-SECOND, you must charge, for all "the troops to your right and left have given way." Three cheers from the regiment expressed the devoted readiness of every individual in its ranks.

The French column did not show a large front. The regiment formed four deep, and in that compact order advanced, until within twenty paces, when it fired a volley, and instantly darted into the heart of the French column, in which it became almost invisible, in the midst of the mass opposed to it.

While the regiment was in the act of charging, and the instant before it came in contact with the enemy, the Scots Greys (second dragoons) came trotting up in rear of its flanks, when both corps shouted "*Scotland for ever!*" the column was instantaneously broken, and in its flight the cavalry rode over it. The result of this dash, which only occupied a few minutes, was a loss to the enemy of two Eagles, and two thousand prisoners, those that escaped doing so without arms or knapsacks.

After this brilliant affair, Sir Denis Pack rode up to the regiment, and said, "You have saved the day "Highlanders, but you must return to your position; "there is more work to be done!!"

It would be superfluous to detail every part that the regiment had to act on this eventful day; how it stood in square, in line, and in column, never yielding an inch to enemies who considered themselves invincible when fighting, as in the present instance, under the direction and in the presence of their Emperor Napoleon Bonaparte, who frequently expressed his astonishment and admiration at the manner in which the British fought, particularly "*Les Braves Ecossais*," as he termed them.

Towards evening two Prussian officers rode past the regiment inquiring for the Duke of Wellington, and their columns began to appear moving upon the enemy's right, by the road from Wavre. At this time the French made a last effort by a general attack throughout the whole line, and the moment they were repulsed, the allied troops advanced, drove them from every position, and forced them to seek safety in flight, leaving their artillery, and everything that constitutes 1815 an army in the field.

The regiment was directed to desist from the pursuit, and return to its original ground, after giving three British cheers to the Prussian army. In this manner was achieved the Battle of Waterloo, the importance of which may be best estimated by the lengthened peace which has ensued; and the memory of this eventful victory will ever survive as a proud monument of the national glory of the British army.

On the 18th of June, the NINETY-SECOND regiment had Captains Peter Wilkie and Archibald Ferrier, Lieutenants Robert Winchester, Donald McDonald, James Ker Ross, and James Hope wounded. Fourteen rank and file were killed, and ninety-six wounded.

In acknowledgment of the services which the army performed in the battle of Waterloo, and the actions immediately preceding it, each subaltern officer and soldier present was permitted to count two years additional service, and silver medals were conferred on all ranks, bearing on the one side an impression of His Royal Highness the Prince Regent, and on the reverse the figure of Victory, holding the palm in the right hand, and the olive branch in the left, with the word "WELLINGTON," over its head, and "WATERLOO," 18th June, 1815, at its feet.

Lieut.-Colonel James Mitchell, who succeeded to the command of the regiment at Quartre Bras, was appointed a companion of the Most Honorable Order of the Bath, and had the Order of St. Anne of Russia conferred upon him. Major Donald McDonald, who commanded the regiment during the whole of the battle of Waterloo, was promoted to the brevet rank of

1815 Lieut.-Colonel, appointed a companion of the Bath, and received the order of St. Wladimir of Russia.

The thanks of both Houses of Parliament were voted to the army with the greatest enthusiasm " for its distinguished valour at Waterloo;" and the NINETY-SECOND, and other regiments engaged, were permitted to bear the word "WATERLOO" on their colours and appointments.

The Highland Society of Scotland unanimously passed a vote of thanks "for the determined valour " and exertions displayed by the regiment, and for the " credit which it did its country in the memorable " battles of the 16th and 18th of June, 1815."

On the 19th of June, the allied army resumed its triumphant pursuit of the French towards Paris, in the neighbourhood of which city the regiment encamped on the 3rd of July, without having been employed on any affair of consequence during the march.

The following General Order was issued by the Duke of Wellington, on the 4th of July:—

" The Field Marshal has great satisfaction in an-
" nouncing to the troops under his command, that he
" has, in concert with Field Marshal Prince Blucher,
" concluded a military convention with the Commander-
" in-Chief of the French army near Paris, by which the
" enemy is to evacuate St. Denis, St. Ouen, Clichy,
" and Neuilly, this day at noon, the heights of Monte
" Martre to-morrow at noon, and Paris next day.

" The Field Marshal congratulates the army upon
" this result of their glorious victory. He desires
" that the troops may employ the leisure of this day
" and to-morrow, to clean their arms, clothes, and ap-
" pointments, as it is his intention that they should
" pass him in review."

Louis XVIII. entered Paris on the 8th of July, and 1815 was once more reinstated on the throne of France. Napoleon Bonaparte having fled to the south of France surrendered himself a prisoner on the 15th of July to Captain Maitland, commanding the "Bellerophon" British ship of war, and the island of St. Helena was afterwards appointed for his residence.

While in camp near Paris, the British army was reviewed by the Emperors of Austria and Russia, and other Sovereigns in alliance with Great Britain, who paid very high compliments to the regiment, and greatly admired its Highland costume.

On the 28th of October, the regiment, under the command of Lieut.-Colonel Mitchell, broke up from its encampment, and marched to St. Germains; on the 30th to Montain Ville; and on the 2nd of November to Neuf le Vieux.

The regiment marched on the 10th of November to occupy the following villages—Monfort, Neuf de Vieux, Creçy, Mareile, and Mere.

The Brigade orders of the 29th of November, directed the regiment to proceed en route to Boulogne, and Major-General Sir Denis Pack, after alluding to the orderly and soldier-like conduct of the regiment both in camp and quarters, and expressing his regret at losing it from under his command, concluded as follows:—

" The services rendered by the NINETY-SECOND
" regiment in the Duke of Wellington's campaigns in
" the Peninsula, and His Grace's late short and
" triumphant one in Belgium, are so generally and so
" highly appreciated, as to make praise from him almost
" idle; nevertheless, he cannot help adding his tri-
" bute of applause."

On the 30th of November, the regiment marched to

1816 Meulan, and arrived on the 15th of December at St. Leonard, near Boulogne; on the 17th it arrived at Calais, and embarked the same day for England.

The effective strength of the regiment consisted of thirty-six serjeants, sixteen drummers, and four hundred and forty-nine rank and file.

On the 19th of December, the regiment landed at Margate; on the 20th marched to Deal; on the 21st to Dover; and on the 22nd to Braebournlees Barracks, from whence it proceeded *en route* to Colchester on the 28th of December.

The regiment arrived at Colchester on the 1st of January, 1816, where an authority was received to reduce its establishment to eight hundred rank and file.

On the 19th of February, the regiment marched from Colchester *en route* to Hull, where it arrived on the 2nd of March. On the 22nd of August, the regiment proceeded to Berwick-upon-Tweed,—from whence it marched to Edinburgh on the 7th of September, and on the 12th went into quarters in Edinburgh Castle, being the second visit to its native country since the original formation of the regiment.

The Grand Duke Nicholas of Russia, having expressed a wish to see the NINETY-SECOND regiment, it was paraded on the 22nd of December accordingly, and His Imperial Highness expressed his admiration of the corps.

1817 On the 7th of April, 1817, the regiment commenced its march by divisions to Port Patrick, there to embark for Ireland. It arrived at Belfast on the 24th of April, and on the 26th, detachments were sent to occupy barracks at Carrickfergus, Downpatrick, Crumlin, Ballimony, Newton Glens, Castle Dawson, Ballycastle, and Randalstown.

Major-General Sir Sidney Beckwith inspected the NINETY-SECOND regiment on the 28th of April, 1818, who issued a very complimentary order regarding its appearance.

On the 17th of June, the regiment commenced its march in two divisions for Castlebar, where the head-quarters arrived on the 28th, having about twenty detachments in various places.

The regiment was inspected on the 14th of October by Major-General Buller, who expressed his approbation of its appearance.

On the 4th of November, orders were received for the regiment to be held in readiness for embarkation at Cork, for Jamaica.

The regiment marched on the 8th of January, 1819, for Fermoy, where it arrived on the 20th of that month. On the 12th of April, it marched from Fermoy to Middleton barracks, and on the following day it embarked, at the Cove of Cork, on board the "Chapman," "Nautilus," and "Ocean" transports. The effective strength consisted of thirty-one serjeants, twenty-one drummers, and six hundred and three rank and file.

On the 14th of April, Major-General Benjamin Gordon expressed "his marked approbation of the "steadiness and very soldier-like appearance of the "regiment, and the regularity with which its embark-"ation was conducted yesterday."

The regiment sailed on the 16th of April, and arrived at Jamaica on the 2nd of June. It disembarked at Kingston on the 4th of that month, and proceeded to Up-Park Camp, followed by the whole population of the town and its vicinity, who crowded from all quarters to witness so novel a sight as a Highland regiment in Jamaica.

1819 Shortly after its arrival in Jamaica, the regiment was attacked by yellow fever in its most virulent form, and three companies, under the command of Brevet Lieut.-Colonel Blainey, marched, on the 5th of July, to Stony Hill barracks.

Such was the mortality and sickness in the regiment, that it was, in August, in a manner ordered to be dispersed. Another company marched on the 26th of August to Stony Hill, and a part of one to the Apostles' battery. On the 28th of August a strong detachment, chiefly composed of convalescents, embarked on board the "Serapis" guard-ship, then at anchor off Port Royal.

Major Archibald Ferrier died at Up-Park-Camp on the 22nd of September, and Brevet Lieut.-Colonel John Blainey having died on the 28th of August at Stony Hill, Brevet-Major Peter Wilkie assumed the command of the regiment, and on the 23rd of September removed with the head-quarters on board the "Serapis." Nothing can depict the state of the regiment better than the following letter from Brevet-Major Wilkie to Lieut.-Colonel Campbell, Assistant Adjutant-General at Jamaica:—

"H. M. Ship Serapis,
"Sir,   25th September, 1819.
" From the very peculiar situation of the
" ninety-second at the present moment, I am much
" afraid it will not be in my power to send in the
" returns required by the different public offices before
" Tuesday or Wednesday next, as having unfortunately
" lost the Adjutant, and every one acquainted with the
" important duty of the orderly room, in the course of
" the present month, I have consequently been necessi-
" tated to take into it any one that could write. Under

"these circumstances, I trust you will grant me all the time you can, to enable me to give them in with some degree of accuracy.

"I have, &c.,
(Signed) "PETER WILKIE,
"*Captain 92nd regiment.*

"Lieut.-Colonel Campbell,
"Assistant Adjutant-General, Jamaica."

The head-quarters were removed on the 9th of November from on board the "Serapis," and returned to Up-Park Camp, where the several detachments joined, and the regiment was again assembled. It was remarked that the men who had been on board ship continued perfectly healthy after their return, whereas those who had been stationed at Stony Hill and the Apostles' Battery, suffered considerably.

The total loss sustained by the regiment from the 25th of June to the 24th of December, 1819, consisted of ten officers,—namely, Majors Archibald Ferrier, and John Blainey (Brevet Lieut.-Colonel), Lieutenants Andrew Will, Thomas Gordon, Hector Innes, George Logan, Richard McDonnell, and George Mackie (Adjutant), Ensign Francis Reynolds, and Assistant Surgeon David Thomas; thirteen serjeants, eight drummers, and two hundred and fifty-four rank and file.

Lieut.-General John Hope was appointed colonel of the NINETY-SECOND on the 29th of January, 1820, in succession to General the Earl of Hopetoun, G.C.B., who was removed to the Forty-second, Royal Highland regiment.

The regiment was inspected on the 16th of February by Major-General Henry Conran, who expressed himself much pleased with the appearance and steadiness of the men under arms.

1820 On the 10th of March, the head-quarters and five companies were removed from Up-Park Camp to Fort Augusta; and on the 14th of that month the other five companies proceeded to Port Royal. In both places the regiment enjoyed comparatively good health.

A detachment of fifty-five rank and file joined the regiment from Scotland on the 24th of May.

Lieut.-Colonel Sir Frederick Stovin, K.C.B., who was promoted from the twenty-eighth to the NINETY-SECOND regiment on the 2nd of September of the previous year, in succession to Lieut.-Colonel James Mitchell, who retired from the service, joined at Jamaica on the 24th of October 1820.

The regimental orders of the 30th of October directed that the dress, on parades and duties, should be white trousers, and that no other dress would be permitted.

On the 21st of December, two companies of the regiment marched from Fort Augusta to Spanish Town.

1821 The head-quarters and three companies at Fort Augusta marched on the 3rd of January, 1821, to Spanish Town, and on the 4th, the five companies at Port Royal were removed to Fort Augusta: one of them was shortly afterwards ordered to join the head-quarters at Spanish Town.

A detachment of one hundred and eighty-five rank and file joined at Jamaica from the regimental depôt on the 13th of January, and on the 5th of February another detachment of twenty-nine joined, making a total of two hundred and fourteen men.

On the 8th of March, the regiment was again inspected by Major-General Henry Conran, commanding the forces at Jamaica, who expressed his approbation of the correct field movements and interior regularity of all its departments.

Lieut.-Colonel Sir Frederick Stovin, having on the 21st of June obtained leave of absence to return to England, Major Peter Wilkie assumed the command of the regiment. On the 18th of August one of the four companies stationed at Fort Augusta marched to join the head-quarters at Spanish Town; and on the 17th of October, the three companies at Fort Augusta, were removed to Port Royal.

1821

On the 24th of October, orders were received from the Secretary at War to reduce the regiment to an establishment of eight companies, consisting of twenty-nine serjeants, twelve drummers, and five hundred and seventy-six rank and file. In consequence of this order, the regiment was formed into eight companies, six being stationed at head-quarters in Spanish Town, and two at Port Royal.

On the 10th of November, a detachment of the regiment, consisting of two subalterns, two serjeants, one drummer, and thirty-two rank and file, embarked for New Providence.

The fifty-eighth and sixty-first regiments being about to return to Europe, a general order was issued on the 28th of November, permitting the men to volunteer to other corps serving in Jamaica; consequently, thirty-three men from the fifty-eighth, and forty-seven from the sixty-first, joined the NINETY-SECOND regiment.

On the 15th of February, 1822, the two companies of the regiment stationed at Port Royal embarked for Port Antonio, where they were detached. On the 19th of February, the head-quarters and three companies marched from Spanish Town, embarked on the same day at Port Henderson, and landed at Falmouth on the 24th of that month; the other three companies embarked shortly afterwards for Montego Bay.

1822

the 10th of February, 1794. He accompanied his regiment to Gibraltar; and on his return to England, he was captured by a French privateer. He afterwards rejoined his regiment at the island of Corsica, where he served upwards of a year; and on the 3rd of May, 1796, he was promoted to the rank of colonel. On the breaking out of the rebellion in Ireland, in 1798, he joined his regiment in that country, where he served as brigadier-general, and was actively employed against the rebels, particularly in Wexford. He accompanied the expedition to Holland in 1799, was at the landing at the Helder, and continued actively employed until the 2nd of October, when he was wounded at the battle of Egmont-op-Zee. On the 1st of January, 1801, he was promoted to the rank of major-general; and in 1803 he was appointed to the staff of North Britain, where he served three years. In January, 1806, he was appointed to the colonelcy of the forty-second, or the Royal Highlanders; and in April, 1808, he was promoted to the rank of lieutenant-general. He commanded a division in the expedition to Holland in 1809; and in August, 1819, he was advanced to the rank of general. In 1820 he was removed to the first,—the Royal Regiment of Foot,—and in a few months afterwards he was nominated a Knight Grand Cross of the Most Honorable Military Order of the Bath. In 1827 he succeeded, on the decease of his father, to the dignity of DUKE OF GORDON: he was also appointed Governor of Edinburgh Castle, and Keeper of the Great Seal of Scotland. In 1834 he was removed to the Scots Fusilier Guards. He was distinguished as a kind-hearted and gallant nobleman and soldier,—contributing largely to many charitable institutions. His social, private, and public virtues, endeared him to his family and friends; and a succession of uninterrupted acts of philanthropy procured him universal esteem. He died on the 28th of May, 1836; and his remains, by especial command of his Majesty King William IV., were escorted by the first battalion of the Scots Fusilier Guards from London to Greenwich, where they were placed on board a steam-vessel, for the purpose of being conveyed to Scotland for interment in a mausoleum erected on the paternal estate. By his Grace's decease the dukedom became extinct.

JOHN, EARL OF HOPETOUN, G.C.B.

Appointed 3rd January, 1806.

THE HONORABLE JOHN HOPE, son of John, second Earl of Hopetoun, evinced a predilection for the profession of arms from his youth, and served as a volunteer in his fifteenth year. On the 28th of May, 1784, he was appointed cornet in the tenth Light Dragoons; two years afterwards, he was nominated lieutenant in the twenty-seventh foot, and in 1789, captain in the seventeenth Light Dragoons; in 1792, he was promoted major in the first foot, and in the following year, lieutenant-colonel in the twenty-fifth regiment, with which corps he served in the West Indies, where he was appointed adjutant-general, and served the campaigns of 1794, 1795, 1796, and 1797, with great distinction, being particularly noticed in the orders and public despatches of Lieutenant-General Sir Ralph Abercromby, and other commanders. In 1796, he was elected a member of parliament for the county of Linlithgow. He was nominated deputy adjutant-general to the expedition to Holland in 1799, and was severely wounded at the landing in North Holland on the 27th of August. In 1800, he was appointed adjutant-general to the army in the Mediterranean, under Lieutenant-General Sir Ralph Abercromby, and served in the expedition to Egypt: he was at the actions of the 8th and 13th of March, 1801, and was wounded before Alexandria on the 21st of March, when Sir Ralph Abercromby received a wound, of which he died on the 28th of March. Brigadier-General Hope recovered, and requesting to have a brigade, was succeeded as adjutant-general by Colonel Abercromby. On the 16th of June, he joined the army before Cairo, with the twenty-eighth and forty-second regiments, and he afterwards evinced ability in conducting the negotiations for the surrender of the capital of Egypt by the French troops, under General Belliard. He continued in the command of a brigade until the deliverance of Egypt was accomplished, and received the second class of the Order of the Crescent established by the Grand Seignior. In 1802, his services were rewarded by the colonelcy of the North Lowland Fencible Infantry, and the rank of major-general; to which was added, in June, 1805, the appointment of deputy-governor of Portsmouth; but he resigned this appointment soon afterwards, to accompany the troops sent to Hanover under Lieutenant-General Lord Cathcart. In October, 1805, he was appointed colonel-commandant of a battalion of the sixtieth regiment; and in 1806, he succeeded the Marquis of Huntly in the colonelcy of the NINETY-SECOND regiment. On the 25th of April, 1808, he was promoted to the rank of lieutenant-general. He was nominated second in command of the expedition to the Baltic, under Lieutenant-General Sir John Moore, and afterwards accompanied the troops to Portugal. He commanded a division of the army which advanced into Spain, under Sir John Moore, and shared in that campaign; and in the battle of Corunna, when he succeeded to the command of the army,—Sir John Moore being killed, and Sir David Baird wounded—he was successful in repulsing the attack of the French under Marshal Soult. On the embarkation of the army, he took particular care to prevent any soldier being left behind, and was the last man who went on board the fleet. His despatch contains an interesting account of the battle.* He was thanked for his distinguished services by parliament, was honored with the approbation of his Sovereign, and the admiration and applause of his country; and was nominated a Knight of the Most Honorable Military Order of the Bath. After his return from Spain, he served with the Walcheren expedition, under General the Earl of Chatham, and was subsequently appointed commander-in-chief in Ireland, from which he was removed, in 1813, to the appointment of second in command in the peninsula. Lieutenant-General SIR JOHN HOPE, commanded the left wing of the army at the battle of the Nivelle on the 10th of November, and signalized himself at the battle of the Nive, in December; on which occasion the British commander stated in his public despatch—" I cannot sufficiently applaud the ability, coolness, " and judgment, of Lieutenant-General Sir John Hope." He passed the Adour with the left wing of the army in February, 1814, and blockaded the important fortress of Bayonne,—in which service he evinced great ability and perseverance: and he remained in the command of the blockading force until the termination of the war. After Napoleon had abdicated, the French commandant at Bayonne

---

* Inserted in Appendix, pages 136 and 137.

not believing the news, made a sortie on the night of the 14th of April, and gained some advantage. Lieutenant-General Sir John Hope coming up with some troops in the dark, encountered the enemy, when his horse being shot, fell upon him, and he was wounded and taken prisoner. The French were, however, repulsed. At the restoration of peace, he returned to England with a high reputation. He received the thanks of parliament; a medal and a clasp for the battles of Corunna and the Nive; was elevated to the peerage of the United Kingdom by the title of Baron Niddry, of Niddry, in the county of Linlithgow, and was nominated a Knight Grand Cross of the Most Honorable Military Order of the Bath. He afterwards succeeded to the dignity of Earl of Hopetoun. In 1819, he was promoted to the rank of General, and was appointed colonel of the forty-second, or the Royal Highlanders, in 1820. He died at Paris on the 27th of August, 1823.

Sir John Hope, G.C.H.

Appointed 29th January, 1820.

John Hope entered the Dutch service, as a cadet, in one of the regiments of the *Scots Brigade* (Houston's) in the service of the United Provinces, in 1778, and served at Bergen-op-Zoom and Maestretcht, going through the subordinate ranks of corporal and serjeant. In 1779 he was appointed ensign, and in 1782 he was promoted captain of a company; but, being called upon to renounce his allegiance to the British monarch, he quitted the Dutch service, and in 1787 he was appointed captain in the sixtieth foot, but his company was soon afterwards reduced. On the 30th of June, 1788, he was appointed captain in the thirteenth Light Dragoons, and in 1792 he was nominated aide-de-camp to Lieut.-General Sir William Erskine, in which capacity he served the campaigns of 1793 and 1794, in Holland, and returned to England in 1795, when he was promoted to the majority of the twenty-eighth Light Dragoons, and in 1796 to the lieut.-colonelcy of the same corps, with which he embarked for the Cape of Good Hope in the same year. He served at the Cape until 1799, when his regiment was incorporated in other corps, and he returned to England. In April, 1799, he was appointed to the thirty-seventh foot, which corps he joined, in 1800, in the West

Indies, where he remained until 1804, when he returned to England, and exchanged to the sixtieth regiment. In 1805 he was nominated assistant adjutant-general in Scotland, and in 1807 he served as deputy adjutant-general to the expedition to Copenhagen, under Lieut.-General Lord Cathcart. He was appointed brigadier-general on the staff of North Britain in 1808, and subsequently deputy adjutant-general in that part of the United Kingdom. He was promoted to the rank of major-general in 1810, and appointed to the staff of the Severn district, from whence he was removed to the staff of the Peninsula in 1812, and served with the army under the Duke of Wellington at the battle of Salamanca, for which he received a medal. He subsequently served on the staff of Ireland and North Britain until 1819, when he was promoted to the rank of lieut.-general. He was honored with the dignity of Knight Grand Cross of the Royal Hanoverian Guelphic Order. In 1820 he was appointed colonel of the NINETY-SECOND regiment, from which he was removed, in 1823, to the seventy-second Highlanders. He died in August 1836.

HONORABLE SIR ALEXANDER DUFF, G.C.H.
Appointed 6th September, 1823.

REMOVED to the thirty-seventh regiment on the 20th of July, 1831.

JOHN EARL OF STAIR, K.T.
Appointed 20th July, 1831.

REMOVED to the forty-sixth regiment on the 31st May, 1843.

SIR WILLIAM MACBEAN, K.C.B.
Appointed 31st May, 1843.

Succession of LIEUTENANT-COLONELS in the NINETY-SECOND Regiment (HIGHLANDERS).

Name.	Date of Appointment.	Date of Removal.	Remarks.
The Marquis of Huntly (*Lieut.-Col. Commandant.*)	10 Feb. 1794	3 May 1796	Promoted Colonel of the NINETY-SECOND Regiment on the 3rd of May, 1796.
Charles Erskine	1 May 1795	..	Died of wounds received in action near *Alexandria*, on the 13th of March, 1801.
James Robertson	11 Oct. 1798	3 Aug. 1804	Retired on half-pay.
Alexander Napier	5 Apr. 1801	..	Killed at the battle of *Corunna*, on the 16th of January, 1809.
James Willoughby Gordon, (*afterwards Quarter-Master Gen. to the Forces*).	4 Aug. 1804	13 June 1808	Promoted Lieut.-Colonel Commandant of the Royal African Corps.
John Cameron	23 June 1808	..	Killed at *Quatre Bras*, on the 16th of June 1815.
John Lamont	30 Mar. 1809	25 Dec. 1814	Retired on half-pay.
James Mitchell	13 June 1815	1 Sept. 1819	Retired.
Sir Frederick Stovin	2 Sept. 1819	8 Aug. 1821	Removed to the 90th foot.
Wm. Brydges Neynoe	9 Aug. 1821	3 Oct. 1821	Exchanged to half-pay of the 4th Foot
David Williamson	4 Oct. 1821	20 Nov. 1828	Retired.
John McDonald	21 Nov. 1828	8 Nov. 1846	Promoted Major-General on the 9th of November, 1846
John Alex. Forbes	9 Nov. 1846	22 Nov. 1849	Retired.
Mark Kerr Atherley	23 Nov. 1849		

Succession of MAJORS of the NINETY-SECOND Regiment (HIGHLANDERS).

Name.	Date of Appointment.	Date of Removal.	Remarks.
Charles Erskine	10 Feb. 1794	30 Apr. 1795	Promoted Lt.-Col. of the NINETY-SECOND regiment.
Donald McDonald	20 Aug. 1794	11 Mar. 1796	Retired.
Simon McDonald	1 May 1795	16 Jan. 1799	Retired.
Alexander Napier	12 Mar. 1796	4 Apr. 1801	Promoted Lt.-Col. of the NINETY-SECOND regiment.
John Gordon	17 Jan. 1799	22 Jan. 1806	Retired.
John Cameron	5 Apr. 1801	22 June 1808	Promoted Lt.-Col. of the NINETY-SECOND regiment.
William Morris	9 July 1803	15 Aug. 1805	Removed to the 8th Veteran Battalion.
Hon. John Ramsay	,,	1 June 1804	Exchanged to half pay.
John Lamont	2 June 1804	29 Mar. 1809	Promoted Lt.-Col. of the NINETY-SECOND regiment.
Archibald McDonnell	29 Aug. 1805	25 Jan. 1813	Promoted Lt.-Col. 13th Veteran Batt.
James Watson	23 Jan. 1806	23 May 1810	Retired
Peter Grant	23 June 1808	25 Nov. 1812	Retired upon full pay.
James Mitchell	30 Mar. 1809	13 June 1815	Promoted Lt.-Col. of the NINETY-SECOND regiment.
Archibald Campbell	24 May 1810	6 Jan. 1813	Retired.
Donald Macdonald	26 Nov. 1812	25 Nov. 1818	Exchanged to half pay of the Malta Regiment.
William Phipps	7 Jan. 1813	25 Dec. 1814	Retired on half pay.
John Macpherson	15 Apr. 1813	. .	Died on 1st January, 1814.
James Seaton	10 Feb. 1814	. .	Died of wounds received in the action at *Garris* on 22nd of March 1814.
James Lee	28 Apr. 1814	25 Dec. 1814	Retired on half pay.
George W. Holmes	18 June 1815	21 Oct. 1818	Retired.

Succession of MAJORS of the NINETY-SECOND Regiment (HIGHLANDERS)—*continued*.

Name.	Date of Appointment.	Date of Removal.	Remarks.
Archibald Ferrier	22 Oct. 1818	. .	Died on the 23rd of September 1819.
John Blainey	26 Nov. 1818	. .	Died on the 28th of August 1819.
Peter Wilkie	4 Nov. 1819	24 Sept 1823	Retired.
George Couper	30 Dec. 1819	19 Mar. 1823	Exchanged to the half pay of the Canadian Fencibles.
James Forrest Fulton	20 Mar. 1823	12 May, 1824	Retired.
Andr. Robt. Charlton	25 Sept. 1823	. .	Died in Aug. 1825.
John Spink	13 May 1824	20 May 1826	Promoted Lt.-Col. Unattached.
Robert Winchester	16 Aug. 1825	31 Oct. 1842	Retired on full pay.
Isaiah Linwood Verity	9 Feb. 1826	21 Mar. 1827	Retired.
Hon. James Sinclair	22 Mar. 1827	18 Feb. 1829	Exchanged to half pay.
Hugh Henry Rose	19 Feb. 1829	16 Sept. 1839	Promoted Lt.-Col. Unattached.
Jno. Alex. Forbes	17 Sept. 1839	8 Nov. 1846	Promoted Lt.-Col. of the NINETY-SECOND regiment.
Geo. Edward Thorold	1 Nov. 1842		
Mark Kerr Atherley	9 Nov. 1846	22 Nov. 1849	Promoted Lt.-Col. of the NINETY-SECOND regiment.
Arch. Inglis Lockhart	23 Nov. 1849		

APPENDIX.

"GENERAL ORDERS. *Horse Guards,*
  16*th May,* 1801.

"THE recent events which have occurred in Egypt have induced His Majesty to lay his most gracious commands on His Royal Highness the Commander-in-Chief, to convey to the troops employed in that country His Majesty's highest approbation of their conduct; and at the same time His Majesty has deemed it expedient that these his gracious sentiments should be communicated to every part of his army, not doubting that all ranks will thereby be inspired with an honorable spirit of emulation, and an eager desire of distinguishing themselves in their country's service.

"Under the blessing of Divine Providence, His Majesty ascribes the successes that have attended the exertions of his troops in Egypt to that determined bravery which is inherent in Britons; but His Majesty desires it may be most solemnly and most forcibly impressed on the consideration of every part of the army, that it has been a strict observance of *order*, *discipline*, and *military* system, which has given its full energy to the native valour of the troops, and has enabled them proudly to assert the superiority of the national military character, in situations uncommonly arduous, and under circumstances of peculiar difficulty.

"The illustrious example of their Commander cannot fail to have made an indelible impression on the gallant troops, at whose head, crowned with victory and glory, he terminated his honorable career; and His Majesty trusts that a due contemplation of the talents and virtues which he uniformly displayed in the course of his valuable life, will for ever endear the memory of SIR RALPH ABERCROMBY to the British army.

"His Royal Highness the Commander-in-Chief having thus obeyed His Majesty's commands, cannot forbear to avail himself of this opportunity of recapitulating the leading features of a series of operations so honorable to the British arms.

"The boldness of the approach to the coast of Aboukir, in defiance of a powerful and well-directed artillery; the orderly formation upon the beach, under the heaviest fire of grape and musketry; the reception and repulse of the enemy's cavalry and infantry; the subsequent charge of our troops, which decided the victory, and established a footing on the shores of Egypt, are circumstances of glory never surpassed in the military annals of the world.

"The advance of the army, on the 13th of March, towards ALEXANDRIA, presents the spectacle of a movement of infantry through an open country, who, being attacked upon their march, *formed*, and *repulsed* the enemy; then advanced in line for three miles, engaged along their whole front, until they drove the enemy to seek his safety under the protection of his entrenched position. Such had been the order and regularity of the advance.

"Upon the 21st of March, the united force of the French in Egypt attacked the position of the British army.

"An attack, begun an hour before daylight, could derive no advantage over the vigilance of an army ever ready to receive it. The enemy's most vigorous and repeated efforts were directed against the right and centre. Our infantry fought in the plain, greatly inferior in the number of their artillery, and unaided by cavalry.

"They relied upon their discipline and their courage. The desperate attacks of a veteran cavalry, joined to those of a numerous infantry, which had vainly styled itself '*Invincible*,' were everywhere repulsed; and a conflict the most severe terminated in one of the most signal victories which ever adorned the annals of the British nation.

"In bringing forward these details, the Commander-in-Chief does not call upon the army merely *to admire* but *to emulate* such conduct. Every soldier who feels for the honor of his country, while he exults in events so splendid and important in themselves, will henceforth have fresh motives for cherishing and enforcing the practice of discipline, and by uniting, in the greatest perfection, order and precision with activity and courage, will seek to uphold, and transmit undiminished to posterity, the *Glory* and *Honor* of the *British Arms*.

"Nor is a less useful example to be derived from the conduct of the distinguished Commander who fell in the field. His steady observance of discipline, his ever-watchful attention to the health and wants of his troops, the persevering and unconquerable spirit which marked his military career, the splendour of his actions in the field, and the heroism of his death, are worthy the imitation of all who desire, like him, a life of honor and a death of glory.

"By Order of His Royal Highness the Commander-in-Chief,

"HARRY CALVERT,
"*Colonel and Adjutant-General.*"

The following Regiments were employed in EGYPT, in 1801, and were permitted by His Majesty King George the Third, to bear on their colours the *Sphinx*, with the word "EGYPT," as a distinguished mark of His Majesty's Royal approbation, and as a lasting memorial of the glory acquired to His Majesty's arms by the zeal, discipline, and intrepidity of his troops in that arduous and important campaign, *viz.*:—

Corps.	Commanding Officers.
‡8th Light Dragoons, 1 Troop	Captain Hawkins.
11th Light Dragoons, 1 Troop	Captain A. Money.
12th ,,	Colonel Mervyn Archdall.
†22nd ,,	Lieut.-Col. Hon. Wm. Lumley.
26th (afterwards 23rd) Light Dragoons.	Lieut.-Colonel Robert Gordon.
Hompesch's Hussars (detachment)	Major Sir Robert T. Wilson.
Coldstream Guards, 1st Battalion	Lieut.-Colonel Arthur Brice.
3rd Foot Guards, 1st Battalion	Lieut.-Colonel T. Hilgrove Turner.
Royals, 2nd Battalion	Lieut.-Colonel Duncan Campbell.
2nd Queen's Royal	Colonel the Earl of Dalhousie.
8th Foot, King's	Colonel Gordon Drummond.
*10th ,,	Lieut.-Colonel Richard Quarrell.
13th ,,	,, Hon. Chas. Colville.
18th, Royal Irish	,, Henry T. Montresor.
†20th Foot, 1st and 2nd Battalions	,, George Smith.
23rd, Royal Welsh Fusiliers	,, John Hall.

APPENDIX.

Corps.	Commanding Officers.
†24th Foot	Lieut.-Colonel John R. Forster.
†25th ,, ...	Colonel William Dyott.
†26th ,, ...	,, Lord Elphinstone.
27th, Inniskilling, 1st & 2nd Bns.	Lieut.-Colonel Samuel Graham.
28th Foot	Colonel Hon. Edward Paget.
30th ,, ...	Lieut.-Colonel Wm. Wilkinson.
40th ,, (Flank Companies) .	Colonel Brent Spencer.
42nd, Royal Highland Regt. .	Lieut.-Colonel William Dickson.
44th Foot	,, David Ogilvie.
50th Foot	Colonel Patrick Wauchope.
54th ,, 1st and 2nd Battalions	Lieut.-Colonel John Thos. Layard.
58th ,, ...	,, William Houston.
‡61st ,, ...	,, Francis Carruthers.
79th ,, ...	Colonel Alan Cameron.
*80th ,, ...	Lieut.-Colonel John Montresor.
*86th ,, ...	,, James P. Lloyd.
*88th ,, ...	Colonel Wm. Carr Beresford.
89th ,, ...	,, William Stewart.
90th ,, ...	,, Rowland Hill.
92nd ,, ...	Lieut.-Colonel Charles Erskine.
†De Watteville's Regiment . .	Lieut.-Col. Louis de Watteville.
The Queen's German Regiment	Lt.-Col. Peter John James Dutens.
De Roll's Regiment	,, The Baron De Dürler.
Dillon's Regiment	,, The Baron Perponcher.
Royal Corsican Rangers . . .	Major Hudson Lowe.
†Ancient Irish Fencibles . . .	
†Chasseurs Britanniques . . .	Colonel John Ramsay.
Staff Corps (detachment).	

* The 10th, 80th, 86th, and 88th Regiments proceeded from the East Indies, under the orders of Major-General David Baird, to join the army in Egypt.

† The 22nd Light Dragoons, 20th (two battalions), 24th, 25th, and 26th Regiments, the Ancient Irish Fencibles, and the foreign corps of De Watteville and Chasseurs Britanniques, joined the Army in Egypt in July, 1801.

‡ One troop of the 8th Light Dragoons and the 61st Regiment, embarked from the Cape of Good Hope, joined the army under Major-General Baird at Cosseir in July, 1801, and proceeded through the Desert to Gheneh, or Kenneh, on the Nile, where the troops embarked for Cairo.

APPENDIX.

List of Regiments which composed the army under Lieut. General Lord Cathcart, employed in the Expedition to COPENHAGEN in the year 1807.

Corps.	Officers.	Men.
Royal Artillery	65	1,545
Royal Engineers	15	53
Coldstream Guards, 1st Battalion	44	1,300
Scots Fusilier Guards ,,	40	1,292
4th Regiment of Foot ,,	46	1,061
7th Royal Fusiliers ,,	37	786
8th Foot ,,	36	859
23rd Royal Welsh Fusiliers ,,	46	1,054
28th Regiment ,,	48	1,158
32nd ,, ,,	36	727
43rd ,, ,,	51	1,065
50th ,, ,,	36	957
52nd ,, 2nd Battalion	31	712
79th ,, 1st Battalion	44	1,044
82nd ,, ,,	38	826
92nd ,, ,,	38	1,039
95th (Rifle Brigade) part of 1st and 2nd Battalions	49	967
Total British	700	16,445

KING'S GERMAN LEGION.

	Officers.	Men.
1st Light Dragoons	36	610
2nd ,,	41	620
3rd ,,	40	621
Royal Artillery	34	675
1st Battalion of the Line	39	824
2nd ,,	38	837
3rd ,,	41	815
4th ,,	41	813
5th ,,	41	802
6th ,,	42	835
7th ,,	39	830
8th ,,	41	726
1st Battalion Light Infantry	40	825
2nd ,,	24	532
Depôt Company	3	130
Garrison Company	2	60
Total King's German Legion	542	10,555
General Total	1,242	27,000

"GENERAL ORDERS.   *His Majesty's Ship,* '*Audacious,*'
18*th January,* 1809.

"The irreparable loss that has been sustained by the fall of the Commander of the Forces (Lieut.-General Sir John Moore), and the severe wound which has removed Lieut.-General Sir David Baird from his station, render it the duty of Lieut.-General Hope to congratulate the army upon the successful result of the action of the 16th instant.

"On no occasion has the undaunted valour of British troop ever been more manifest. At the termination of a severe and harassing march, rendered necessary by the superiority which the enemy had acquired, and which had materially impaired the efficiency of the troops, many disadvantages were to be encountered.

"These have all been surmounted by the conduct of the troops themselves; and the enemy has been taught, that whatever advantages of position, or of numbers he may employ, there is inherent in the British officers and soldiers, a bravery that knows not how to yield, that no circumstances can appal, and that will ensure victory when it is to be obtained by the exertion of any human means.

"The Lieut.-General has the greatest satisfaction in distinguishing such meritorious services, as came within his observation, or have been brought to his knowledge.

"His acknowledgments are, in a peculiar manner, due to Lieut.-General Lord William Bentinck, and the brigade under his command, consisting of the fourth, forty-second, and fiftieth regiments, and which sustained the weight of the attack.

"Major-General Manningham, with his brigade, consisting of the Royals, the twenty-sixth and eighty-first regiments, and Major-General Warde, with the brigade of Guards, will also be pleased to accept his best thanks for their steady and gallant conduct during the action.

"To Major-General Paget, who, by a judicious movement of the reserve, effectually contributed to check the progress of the enemy on the right; and to the first battalion of the fifty-second and ninety-fifth regiments, which were thereby engaged, the greatest praise is justly due.

"That part of Major-General Leith's brigade which was engaged, consisting of the fifty-ninth regiment, under the conduct of the Major-General, also claims marked approbation.

"The enemy not having rendered the attack on the left a serious one, did not afford to the troops stationed in that quarter an opportunity of displaying that gallantry which must have made him repent the attempt.

"The piquets and advanced posts, however, of the brigades under the command of *Major-Generals Hill and Leith*, and *Colonel Catlin Craufurd*, conducted themselves with determined resolution; and were ably supported by the officers commanding these brigades, and by the troops of which they were composed.

"It is peculiarly incumbent upon the Lieut.-General to notice the vigorous attack made by the second battalion of the *fourteenth* regiment under *Lieut.-Colonel Nicolls*, which drove the enemy out of the village, of the left of which he had possessed himself.

"The exertions of *Lieut.-Colonel Murray*, Quarter-Master General, and of the other officers of the General Staff, during the action, were unremitted, and deserve every degree of approbation.

"The illness of *Brigadier-General Clinton*, Adjutant-General, unfortunately deprived the army of the benefit of his services.

"The Lieut.-General hopes the loss in point of numbers is not so considerable as might have been expected; he laments, however, the fall of the gallant soldiers and valuable officers who have suffered.

"The Lieut.-General knows that it is impossible, in any language he can use, to enhance the esteem, or diminish the regret, that the army feels with him for its late Commander His career has been unfortunately too limited for his country, but has been sufficient for his own fame. Beloved by the army, honored by his Sovereign, and respected by his country, he has terminated a life devoted to her service, by a glorious death,—leaving his name as a memorial, an example, and an incitement, to those who shall follow him in the path of honor, and it is from his country alone that his memory can receive the tribute which is its due.

(Signed)   " JOHN HOPE, *Lieut.-General.*"

" GENERAL ORDERS.   *Horse Guards,*
                        1*st February,* 1809.

" The benefits derived to an army from the example of a distinguished Commander, do not terminate at his death; his virtues live in the recollection of his associates, and his fame remains the strongest incentive to great and glorious actions.

" In this view, the Commander-in-Chief, amidst the deep and universal regret which the death of Lieut.-General Sir JOHN MOORE has occasioned, recalls to the troops the military career of that illustrious officer for their instruction and imitation.

" Sir JOHN MOORE from his youth embraced the profession with the feelings and sentiments of a soldier; he felt that a perfect knowledge, and an exact performance of the humble, but important duties of a subaltern officer, are the best foundations for subsequent military fame; and his ardent mind, while it looked forward to those brilliant achievements for which it was formed, applied itself, with energy and exemplary assiduity, to the duties of that station.

" In the school of regimental duty, he obtained that correct knowledge of his profession so essential to the proper direction of the gallant spirit of the soldier; and he was enabled to establish a characteristic order and regularity of conduct, because the troops found in their leader a striking example of the discipline which he enforced on others.

" Having risen to command, he signalized his name in the West Indies, in Holland, and in Egypt. The unremitting attention with which he devoted himself to the duties of every branch of his profession, obtained him the confidence of Sir Ralph Abercromby, and he became the companion in arms of that illustrious officer, who fell at the head of his victorious troops, in an action which maintained our national superiority over the arms of France.

" Thus Sir JOHN MOORE at an early period obtained, with general approbation, that conspicuous station, in which he gloriously terminated his useful and honorable life.

" In a military character obtained amidst the dangers of climate, the privations incident to service, and the sufferings of repeated wounds, it is difficult to select any one point as a preferable subject for praise; it exhibits, however, one feature so particularly characteristic of the man, and so important to the best interests of the service, that the Commander-in-Chief is pleased to mark it with his peculiar approbation—

"THE LIFE OF SIR JOHN MOORE WAS SPENT AMONG THE TROOPS.

"During the season of repose, his time was devoted to the care and instruction of the officer and soldier; in war he courted service in every quarter of the globe. Regardless of personal considerations, he esteemed that to which his country called him, *the post of honor*, and by his undaunted spirit and unconquerable perseverance, he pointed the way to victory.

"His country, the object of his latest solicitude, will rear a monument to his lamented memory, and the Commander-in-Chief feels he is paying the best tribute to his fame by thus holding him forth as an EXAMPLE to the ARMY.

"By order of His Royal Highness the Commander-in-Chief,

"HARRY CALVERT, *Adjutant-General*."

APPENDIX.

The following Regiments composed the Army under Lieut.-General Sir JOHN MOORE, at CORUNNA, on the 16th January, 1809.

Corps.	Commanding Officers.
7th Light Dragoons	Lieut.-Colonel Vivian.
10th ,,	,, Leigh.
15th ,,	,, Grant.
18th ,,	,, Jones.
3rd ,, (King's Germ. Leg.)	Major Burgwesel.
Artillery	Colonel Harding.
Engineers	Major Fletcher.
Waggon Train Detachment	Lieut.-Colonel Langley.
1st Foot Guards, 1st Battalion	,, Cocks.
,, 3rd ,,	,, Wheatley.
1st Foot . . 3rd ,,	Major Muller.
2nd ,, . . 1st ,,	Lieut.-Colonel Iremonger.
4th ,, . . 1st ,,	,, Wynch.
5th ,, . . 1st ,,	,, Mackenzie.
6th ,, . . 1st ,,	Major Gordon.
9th ,, . . 1st ,,	Lieut.-Colonel Cameron.
14th ,, . . 2nd ,,	,, Nicolls.
20th ,, . . ,,	,, Ross.
23rd ,, . . 2nd ,,	,, Wyatt.
26th ,, . . 1st ,,	,, Maxwell.
28th ,, . . 1st ,,	, Belson.
32nd ,, . . 1st ,,	,, Hinde.
36th ,, . . 1st ,,	,, Burn.
38th ,, . . 1st ,,	,, Hon. Chas. Greville.
42nd ,, . . 1st ,,	,, Stirling.
43rd ,, . . 1st ,,	,, Gifford.
43rd ,, . . 2nd ,,	,, Hull.
50th ,, . . 1st ,,	Major Charles Napier.
51st ,, . . ,,	Lieut.-Colonel Darling.
52nd ,, . . 1st ,,	,, Barclay.
52nd ,, . . 2nd ,,	,, John Ross.
59th ,, . . 2nd ,,	,, Fane.
60th ,, . . 2nd ,,	,, Codd.
60th ,, . . 5th ,,	Major Davy.
71st ,, . . 1st ,,	Lieut.-Colonel Pack.
76th ,, . . 1st ,,	,, Symes.
79th ,, . . 1st ,,	,, Cameron.
81st ,, . . 2nd ,,	Major Williams.
82nd ,, . . ,,	,, M'Donald.
91st ,, . . 1st ,,	,, Douglas.
92nd ,, . . 1st ,,	Lieut.-Colonel Alexander Napier.
95th (Rifle Reg.) 1st ,,	,, Beckwith.
,, ,, 2nd ,,	,, Wade.
Staff Corps Detachment	,, Nicolay.
1st Light Batt. King's German Legion.	,, Leonhart.
2nd ,,	,, Halkett.

APPENDIX.

BRITISH AND HANOVERIAN ARMY AT WATERLOO
as formed in Divisions and Brigades on the 18th of June, 1815.

CAVALRY.

Commanded by Lieut.-General the EARL OF UXBRIDGE G.C.B.

1st Brigade.—Commanded by Major-General LORD EDWARD SOMERSET, K.C.B.

1st Life Guards	Lieut.-Colonel Ferrior.
2nd ,,	,, the Hon. E.P. Lygon.
Royal Horse Guards, Blue	,, Sir Robert Hill.
1st Dragoon Guards	,, Fuller (Colonel).

2nd Brigade.—Major-General SIR WILLIAM PONSONBY, K.C.B.

1st or Royal Dragoons.	Lieut.-Colonel, A. B. Clifton.
2nd or Royal North British Dragoons	,, J. J. Hamilton.
6th or Inniskilling Dragoons	,, J. Muter (Colonel).

3rd Brigade.—Major-General W. B. DORNBERG.

23rd Light Dragoons	Lieut.-Colonel the Earl of Portarlington (Colonel).
1st ,, King's German Legion	,, J. Bulow.
2nd ,, ,,	,, C. de Jonquiera.

4th Brigade.—Major-General SIR JOHN O. VANDELEUR, K.C.B.

11th Light Dragoons	Lieut.-Colonel J. W. Sleigh.
12th ,,	,, the Honorable F. C. Ponsonby (Colonel).
16th ,,	,, J. Hay.

5th Brigade.—Major-General SIR COLQUHOUN GRANT, K.C.B.

7th Hussars	Colonel Sir Edward Kerrison
15th ,,	Lieut.-Colonel L. C. Dalrymple.
2nd ,, King's German Legion.	,, Linsingen.

6th Brigade.—Major-General SIR HUSSEY VIVIAN, K.C.B.

10th Royal Hussars.	Lieut.-Colonel Quentin (Colonel).
18th Hussars.	,, Hon. H. Murray.
1st ,, King's German Legion.	,, A. Wissell.

7th Brigade.—Colonel SIR FREDERICK ARENSCHILDT, K.C.B.

13th Light Dragoons.	Lieut.-Colonel Doherty.
3rd Hussars King's German Legion.	,, Meyer.

Colonel ESTORFF.

Prince Regent's Hussars.	Lieut.-Colonel Kielmansegge.
Bremen and Verden Hussars	Colonel Busche.

APPENDIX.

INFANTRY.

First Division.—Major-General G. Cooke.

1st Brigade.—Major-General P. Maitland.

1st Foot Guards, 2nd Battalion.	Major H. Askew (Colonel).
,, 3rd ,,	,, the Honorable W. Stewart (Colonel)

2nd Brigade.—Major-General J. Byng.

Coldstream Guards, 2nd Battalion.	Major A. G. Woodford (Colonel).
3rd Foot Guards, ,,	,, F. Hepburn (Colonel).

Second Division.—Lieut.-General Sir H. Clinton, G.C.B.

3rd Brigade.—Major-General F. Adam.

52nd Foot, 1st Battalion.	Lieut.-Colonel Sir John Colborne, K.C.B. (Colonel).
71st ,, ,,	,, T. Reynell (Col.)
95th ,, 2nd ,, } Rifles.	Major J. Ross (Lieut.-Colonel).
95th ,, 3rd ,,	Major A. G. Norcott (Lieut.-Col.)

1st Brigade, King's German Legion.—Colonel Du Plat.

1st Line Battalion, King's German Legion	Major W. Robertson.
2nd ,, ,,	,, G. Muller.
3rd ,, ,,	Lieut.-Colonel F. de Wissell.
4th ,, ,,	Major F. Reh.

3rd Hanoverian Brigade.—Colonel Halkett.

Militia Battalion Bremervorde	Lieut.-Colonel Schulenberg.
Duke of York's 2nd Battalion.	Major Count Munster.
,, 3rd ,,	,, Baron Hunefeld.
Militia Battalion Salzgitter	,, Hammerstein.

Third Division.—Lieut.-General Baron Alten.

5th Brigade.—Major-General Sir Colin Halkett, K.C.B.

30th Foot, 2nd Battalion.	Major W. Bailey (Lieut.-Colonel).
33rd ,,	Lieut.-Colonel W. K. Elphinstone.
69th ,, 2nd Battalion.	,, C. Morice (Col.)
73rd ,, 2nd Battalion.	,, W. G. Harris (Colonel).

2nd Brigade.—King's German Legion.—Colonel Baron Ompteda.

1st Light Battalion, K.G.L.	Lieut.-Colonel L. Bussche.
2nd ,, ,,	Major G. Baring.
5th Line ,, ,,	Lieut.-Colonel W. B. Linsingen.
8th ,, ,, ,,	Major Schroeder (Lieut.-Colonel).

1st Hanoverian Brigade.—Major-General Count Kielmansegge.

Duke of York's 1st Battalion.	Major Bulow.
Field Battalion Grubenhagen.	Lieut.-Colonel Wurmb.
,, Bremen	,, Langrehr.
,, Luneburg.	,, Kleucke.
,, Verden.	Major De Senkopp.

APPENDIX.

FOURTH DIVISION.—Lieut.-General SIR CHARLES COLVILLE, K.C.B.

4th Brigade.—Colonel MITCHELL.

14th Foot, 3rd Battalion.	Major F. S. Tidy (Lieut.-Col.)
23rd ,, 1st ,,	Lieut.-Colonel Sir Henry W. Ellis, K.C.B.
51st ,, ,,	,, H. Mitchell (Colonel).

6th Brigade.—Major-General JOHNSTONE.

35th Foot, 2nd Battalion.	Major C. M'Alister.
54th ,,	Lieut.-Col. J. Earl of Waldegrave.
59th ,, 2nd Battalion.	,, H. Austin.
91st ,, 1st ,,	,, Sir W. Douglas, K.C.B., (Colonel).

6th Hanoverian Brigade.—Major-General LYON.

Field Battalion, Calenberg.	
,, Lanenberg.	Lieut.-Colonel Benort.
Militia Battalion, Hoya.	,, Grote.
,, Nienberg.	
,, Bentheim.	Major Croupp.

FIFTH DIVISION.—Lieut.-General SIR THOMAS PICTON, K.C.B.

5th Brigade.—Major-General SIR JAMES KEMPT, K.C.B.

28th Foot, 1st Battalion.	Major R. Nixon (Lieut.-Colonel).
32nd ,, ,,	,, J. Hicks (Lieut.-Colonel).
79th ,, ,,	Lieut.-Colonel Neil Douglas.
95th Rifles ,,	,, Sir A. F. Barnard, K.C.B., (Colonel).

9th Brigade.—Major-General SIR DENIS PACK, K.C.B.

1st Foot, 3rd Battalion.	Major C. Campbell.
42nd ,, 1st ,,	Lieut.-Colonel Sir Robert Macara, K.C.B.
44th ,, 2nd ,,	,, J. M. Hamerton.
92nd ,, 1st ,,	Major Donald M'Donald.

5th Hanoverian Brigade.—Colonel VINCKE.

Militia Battalion, Hameln.	Lieut.-Colonel Kleucke.
,, Hildesheim.	Major Rheden.
,, Peina.	Major Westphalen.
,, Giffhorn.	Major Hammerstein.

SIXTH DIVISION.—10th Brigade.—Major-General J. LAMBERT.

4th Foot, 1st Battalion.	Lieut.-Colonel F. Brooke.
27th ,, ,,	Captain Sir J. Reade (Major).
40th ,, ,,	Major F. Browne.
81st ,, 2nd ,,	,, P. Waterhouse.

4th Hanoverian Brigade.—Colonel BEST.

Militia Battalion,	Luneburg.	Lieut.-Colonel De Ramdohr.
,,	Verden.	Major Decken.
,,	Osterode.	,, Baron Reden.
,,	Minden.	,, De Schmidt.

7th Brigade.—Major-General M'KENZIE.

25th Foot, 2nd Battalion.		Lieut.-Colonel A. W. Light.
37th ,, ,,		,, S. Hart.
78th ,, ,,		,, M. Lindsay.

Cavalry 8,883
Infantry 29,622
Artillery 5,434
Total 43,939

LONDON:
Printed by W. CLOWES and SONS, Stamford Street,
For Her Majesty's Stationery Office.